"Ruth Buezis offers such an authentic understanding of sexual connection in marriage. Overflowing with God's truths about sex, as well as her own story and the genuine stories of other women, *Awaken Love* unpacks the conversations women long to have. If you have wrestled with getting at the heart of what it takes to enjoy and nurture sex in your marriage, this book is a must read." -- JULIE SIBERT, author of *Pursuit of Passion* and founder of IntimacyInMarriage.com.

"When I started reading *Awaken Love* I thought, 'Wow, this is good! How do I buy copies for all my friends?' In sharing her story, Ruth addresses the fears and lies we believe about sex. I found myself working through each of them to let them slip away and step more firmly into God's truth about His good gift of sex. The book covers topics including the purpose of sex, body image, dealing with porn and sexual freedom within God's guidelines, making it an amazing tool in the battle for healthy sex in marriage." -- LORI BYERLY, co-founder of TheMarriageBed.com and author of TheGenerousWife.com.

"In *Awaken Love*, Ruth Buezis asks us all to take an honest look at our own views of sex and sexuality. Her gentle transparency invites us into the process of sexual growth and inspires us to embrace the joys of the marriage bed." – CHRIS TAYLOR, author of TheForgivenWife.com.

"Ruth's knowledge and passion for such a delicate topic will not only change your sex life, it will change the way you view intimacy, period. It is so clear that God has anointed her to 'awaken love' within Christian marriages, and because of this, there's just no way you can read her book and not be transformed!" – JONNA MEIDAL, author of Jonnameidal.com.

# AWAKEN
# LOVE

## THE TRUTH ABOUT SEX THAT WILL
## TRANSFORM YOUR MARRIAGE

Ruth Buezis

The advice and strategies contained in herein may not be suitable for your situation. This book is not intended as a substitute for therapy or medical advice of a physician. The reader should regularly consult a therapist, psychiatrist, or physician in matters relating to his or her mental or physical health and particularly with respect to any symptoms that may require diagnosis or medical attention.

Names and identifying details have been changed to protect the privacy of individuals.

All Scripture quotations, unless otherwise indicated, are taken from the Holy Bible, New International Version®, NIV®. Copyright ©1973, 1978, 1984, 2011 by Biblica, Inc.™ Used by permission of Zondervan. All rights reserved worldwide. www.zondervan.com The "NIV" and "New International Version" are trademarks registered in the United States Patent and Trademark Office by Biblica, Inc.™

Scriptures marked KJV are taken from the KING JAMES VERSION (KJV): KING JAMES VERSION, public domain.

For information on distribution or for questions contact the author at www.awaken-love.net.

Minneapolis, Minnesota 55441

Book Layout ©2017 BookDesignTemplates.com

Illustrations by Ruth and Sarah Buezis

Awaken-Love: the truth about sex that will transform your marriage/Ruth Buezis. —1st ed.

ISBN 978-1-7324459-0-1

*To Jim*
*You never gave up on me, held me in the depths of my*
*insecurities and matched me in every step of growth.*
*You have been my rock and I love you.*

*To Grace, Mattie, Anne and Sarah*
*Thank you for not freaking out when your mom decided to*
*teach sex classes on the back porch. I pray that when the*
*time is right, you will have the courage to read my story.*

# Contents

# Acknowledgements

*When Moses' hands grew tired, they took a stone and put it under him and he sat on it. Aaron and Hur held his hands up—one on one side, one on the other.  (Exodus 17:12)*

So many amazing women have held up my hands as I shared the truth about sex. Women in classes trusted me with their stories and spurred me on to keep teaching. Tiffany showed me what it looks like to live a life surrendered to God. My prayer team interceded as I experienced the highs and lows of the battle for sexuality. Gifted women joined me when God called them to teach Awaken-Love at their churches. Melanie walked along side of me and poured 2 years into making the women's video class and solidifying the ministry. Jessie, Beth and Melody caught me when I was ready to give up. Sarah and Tracy provided direction and unfailing encouragement. Becky, Chris and Jonna helped edit a book that I never imagined possible. God just kept bringing women to hold up my hands.

Through all the ups and downs, God never left my side. He met me in the excitement, the trenches and when I felt like I just had all the wind knocked out of me. God opened door after door from the time I prayed "even if it is only one", to the day I prayed, "even if it is thousands".

God, thank you for always showing up. You are so faithful and you are worthy to be praised.

# CHAPTER 1

# Transformation

MOST PEOPLE UNDERSTAND how destructive sex can be. We all know families torn apart after the betrayal of infidelity. Many of us crossed lines before marriage that filled us with shame, regret, or resentment. The lure of porn has caused deceit and lies in our marriages; it has broken trust and distorted sex. It's easy to feel like all we want to do is protect ourselves and our sons and daughters. While sex outside of God's boundaries can cause enormous pain, sex within God's design has the power to transform your marriage.

Few wives understand how powerfully *good* sex can be. We cannot comprehend how sex could possibly connect us to our husbands in the midst of conflict. Few of us have allowed our husbands to comfort us by making love after loss or disappointment. When stress or exhaustion wears us down, we cannot fathom that lying skin to skin with our husbands might be exactly what we need. We reduce sex to a physical response rather than see it as a holy experience of learning about true intimacy. Instead of embracing sex as a powerful gift from God we buy into what culture has taught us.

The world treats sex as a commodity to sell things or get what we want. Messages from the church focus on purity or on the needs of men. Silence from our parents or the church makes us feel like sex, even within marriage, is somehow dirty or wrong. These messages, along with our past experiences twist how we feel about sex. They distort how we see our husbands, ourselves and how we view sex.

When you strip away all of the lies, shame, and silence, you begin to understand God's *original* intent for sex in marriage, and you find something *radically* different. God intended sex to be this amazing gift for both husbands *and* wives, but it isn't easy. Contrary to what the movies portray, great sex doesn't just happen. Creating a sex life that gets better and better with each year of marriage will take courage.

## Change

I love the story of Jesus's encounter with the paralytic man near the pool of Bethesda.

> When Jesus saw him lying there and learned that he had been in this condition for a long time, he asked him, "Do you want to get well?" "Sir", the invalid replied, "I have no one to help me into the pool when the water is stirred. While I am trying to get in, someone else goes down ahead of me". Then Jesus said to him, "Get up! Pick up your mat and walk." (John 5:6-8)

The first question we ask ourselves is, "**Do I want to get well?**" Do we even realize that we aren't well? God wants us to have a marriage and sex life more intimate than we could ever imagine. He wants it to be filled with growth and depth and new discoveries. So many of us have settled for the status quo for years because we're afraid to rock the boat or experience rejection. We convince ourselves that intimate, sizzling marriages don't even exist.

For Tessa, sex had been a disappointment since her honeymoon. As we read Song of Songs in class, her face gradually hardened until she finally erupted, "That's a fairy tale! That doesn't happen in real life." I gently reminded her, "This is God's Word. You may not have experienced anything close to this and I am so sorry. But this, this is what God wants for you and for your marriage."

We have to wrap our minds around what God *wants* for us before we can go after it. Our prize must outweigh our fear. Our desire for freedom must overcome our need for safety. Creating an amazing sex life in your marriage will require you to grow, and the desire to "get well" is the first step towards transformation.

After Jesus asked the man if he wanted to get well, the invalid replied, "I have no one to help me into the pool when the water is stirred. While I am trying to get in, someone else goes down ahead of me." (John 5:7)

Just like the invalid, we have no problem coming up with excuses to avoid working on our sex life:

*I don't have time.*

*Sex does nothing for me.*

*I need to take care of the kids.*

*I don't need to dredge that pain up again.*

*All he cares about is sex.*

*I can't compete with those women.*

*I can't talk about that!*

We will use *any* excuse to avoid working on our sex life. Regardless of our situation, we can create more intimacy in our marriage. Though we cannot change our husbands, we *can* change ourselves. When we decide to be more open and vulnerable, our marriages become more intimate regardless of our husbands' actions. Transformation will not happen until we stop making excuses.

Then Jesus said to the invalid, "Get up! Pick up your mat and walk." (John 5:8)

Just like the invalid, we must have faith to believe that change can happen. To **"get up"** when we feel paralyzed.

When a friend invited Carly to class, her heart immediately began to race. The thought of tackling the one area in her marriage that caused constant conflict terrified her, but she knew she had to do something. After years of dreading sex, she was ready to dive in and figure things out.

We must get outside of our comfort zone and try something different. Rather than hanging onto our old mindset and patterns we must learn new ways to both think and act.

Then Jesus tells us to **"pick up our mat"**, a remembrance of where we came from. Rather than deny our sexual baggage we learn from it. Instead of forgetting our past we share our testimonies of God's healing and redemption. Our stories will spur others on towards greater growth, freedom and faith. People need to know that God cares about our sexuality.

The invalid then "walked" out his faith and we must **"walk"** out ours. God heals us from past experiences to *set us free*. He wants to give us a taste of the Garden of Eden where we can explore wide-open spaces, naked and unashamed. God is offering us deeper intimacy with our husband and with Him. Will you receive it?

I don't know the details of your marriage or the challenges that you face, but I know that we serve a powerful God. He is able to do more than you could ever ask or imagine. Nothing about your sex life exists that will shock Him or that He cannot handle.

## A Little Encouragement

You may feel overwhelmed with the ideas in this book, and it might feel like you've had a firehose aimed at your face. Take time to digest everything and realize that change happens one baby step at a time. Whether that involves writing out lies you've believed about sex, sorting through your baggage, learning to orgasm, or communicating your needs during sex, just focus on one small step. A few *Action Items* follow each chapter to help you move from head knowledge to heart knowledge, but you will never arrive. We will always have new things to discover about intimacy in marriage.

More than anything, I hope that you have a new understanding of who God is and how much we need Him. I like to say that marriage, and especially sex, is this amazing people-growing machine. Working on your marriage and your sex life will challenge and grow your faith as you ask Him for transformation.

I don't want to imply that sex is the answer to all marital struggles. Jesus is. Sex will not fix a broken marriage. Every suggestion I make assumes that you have a loving husband. God does not condone tolerating an abusive relationship or not setting healthy boundaries with your husband. God tells husbands to love their wives by laying down their own lives. If your marriage feels unsafe, I implore you to tell someone and seek help.

## Final Thoughts

Whether or not you can put His truth into practice in your marriage today, God wants you to know his intention for sex. If you were a virgin bride disillusioned because following the rules didn't lead to a fairy tale honeymoon or if you wonder what happened after 25 years of "going through the motions", Jesus has the answers. It doesn't matter if you've suffered sexual abuse or can't count how many men you've slept with, God wants you to be whole. Whether you hate having sex or you want sex more often than your husband, God wants you to experience freedom. If you have been seduced by the offerings of the world, erotica, porn, or whatever else you can imagine, God wants you to experience true intimacy. Whatever your situation, I pray that God's truth would resonate with your soul and that this book leads you to His answers.

God has taken me on the ride of my life and has stretched me to believe in the impossible. He has given me a front row seat to watch women transform the most pain-filled, vulnerable parts of their lives—their sexuality—into something that brings them life. God has completely changed me and my marriage.

I pray that God uses my story, and the lives of other women, to open your eyes to the gift He has for you. I pray that you will not only have the courage to transform your life but that you will begin to speak the truth to your husband, your children, your friends, and your church. It is time to start talking about sex—the full story—without limits. Our world desperately needs to know the truth.

## Action Items

1. Make a list of the ways that you have witnessed or heard that sex is destructive? How does that make you feel?
2. What excuses do you tend to use when you don't want to make your sex life a priority?

# CHAPTER 2

# My Story

JIM AND I HAVE BEEN MARRIED for over thirty years and have raised four amazing daughters. As a couple of left-brained engineers, we had a comfortable marriage grounded in common interests and activities. Rather than sharing our thoughts or feelings, we lived a safe, predictable life based on what we did. Even though we knew God, it was more head knowledge than an intimate relationship. We went to church but rarely prayed together or shared what God was doing in our lives. We enjoyed sex on my terms and my schedule. Early on in our marriage, we figured out what worked and stuck with it. We had no idea how to communicate or even connect during sex. For me, sex felt like going through the motions simply to satisfy a physical urge. So you can imagine that I never thought in a million years I would one day teach sex classes!

In 2010, God woke me during a study on Song of Songs. Every week our homework included reading the entire book of Song of Songs out loud and journaling about a different dimension of our relationship with God. I remember feeling shocked and timid as these words—so sweet, raw and naked—soaked into my soul. As I awoke to the love of God, I changed.

I let myself feel, live, and awaken. Worship became a place to pour myself out and meet with God. I found words of praise randomly bursting from my lips as prayer transformed to a constant conversation with God. Instead of running from pain-filled situations, I entered *into* them. I probably cried more that year than in the previous forty years put together. I was no longer content to hide, and people started saying to me, "You look different. What's going on?"

My transformation also impacted my marriage. I remember after several weeks of the study saying to my husband, "Do you know how many times we have had sex in the last couple of weeks?" I not only hungered for more intimacy with God, but with Jim too. I intuitively knew that working on our sex life was part of the answer to creating an intimate marriage, even though by most standards, we already had a good marriage. But God wanted us to have an amazing marriage! The kind of marriage where your kids look at you and say, "I want that!"

First, I went searching for answers about God's design for sex. The Song of Songs—eight beautiful chapters in the Bible—became my guide for marital intimacy. God portrayed this passionate, mutually enjoyable love affair that drastically contrasted with how I felt about sex.

Next, I uncovered lies that I believed about myself, my husband, and sex. These lies came not only from the world but also from the church. I dug up sexual baggage that impacted my freedom. I experienced God's amazing healing. I even went after answers about how my body works, how my husband's body works, and how they work together.

Finally, I had to take steps of faith in order to live out my new-found freedom. I ventured into the unknown and allowed myself to express deep needs and desires. I tapped into my God-given creativity and sensuality and discovered what an amazing body God gave me. Over and over, I got naked as I shared myself physically, emotionally, and spiritually with my husband.

*Discuss with your husband what creates intimacy in your marriage. How would your kids describe a marriage they look forward to?*

## Dependence on God

Working on my sex life has been one of the hardest things I have ever done, and it has caused me to depend on God.

I remember one night in particular when I felt frustrated with our lack of connection. As my husband snored, I lay awake tossing and turning. Finally, I dragged myself out of bed, slipped on my coat, pulled up my boots, and went out to shovel the foot of snow blanketing our driveway. As I blew off steam, my head replayed over and over the events that evening. Shoveling brought release, and the beauty of the snow softened my heart until I suddenly realized I was singing worship songs. In an instant, a light bulb went off in my head.

My husband could never make me happy or meet all of my needs. As hard as he tried, my poor husband didn't have a chance. Only God could fill the empty hole in my soul.

Working on your sex life will require you to get naked over, and over, and over again. It will require you to open up the deepest parts of your soul and let someone see you—all your faults, insecurities, wild crazy ideas, and turn-ons. Your spouse will let you down. No matter how much your husband loves you or how hard he tries, he will let you down. He will react the wrong way, say the wrong thing, or even look at you the wrong way—not because he wants to hurt you, but because he is human.

Your gut reaction will be to jerk back into hiding. If you want to keep creating intimacy, then you better hang onto God.

Christians often use the phrase, "Get your worth from God." Sex will put it to the test. If you depend on your husband's reaction during sex, then you may just give up. In order to vulnerably share yourself during sex, you must have a steadiness that comes from knowing who God created you to be. Regardless of whether your spouse reacts the right ways or exposes himself as much as you do, you get naked because God calls us to be known.

I used to be afraid of letting anyone know me. I had a reputation to uphold. I was the good girl, the responsible one, the steady one. The more I realized just how broken I was and incapable of doing anything on my own, the more I realized I have nothing to lose. If I accomplish anything, it is because of God, not me. There is a freedom that comes from being fully known—to God, to our husbands, and even to friends. When we stop hiding, we start living.

If nothing else comes out of reading this book or from working on your sex life, I pray that you discover Jesus Christ.

Without Him, all of this is pointless anyway. He is the one who changes lives. He is the one who will set you free.

## Preparation

After experiencing profound growth that year, God called me to do the unthinkable—share what I had learned about sex with other women. While researching Christian resources about sex, I discovered an entire world on the internet made up of Christian blogs and forums. Under the anonymity of the internet, women asked questions, shared suggestions, and encouraged each other. Reading the comments not only inspired me to press on, it also opened a window into how many Christian women struggled with sex. I knew I had to do something but had no idea what.

I remember wrestling all night with God at a women's retreat in the fall of 2011. I had no formal training, was terrified of public speaking, and shied away from emotional situations. How could He possibly expect *me* to address the importance of sex in marriage? Somewhere in the back of my head, I knew that God was calling me to teach about sex. If I didn't tell someone about it soon, I would talk myself out of it. Better yet, I would convince myself I had imagined the entire thing!

So the next morning, during an early morning walk with a close friend, I took a deep breath and gathered my courage. I told her how God had changed my marriage and that I believed God was calling me to teach about the importance of sex in Christian marriages. As I shared my excitement about this newfound intimacy with my husband, my friend tearfully admitted she and her husband had been struggling. For the next six months, I shared more of what God had taught me, suggesting fun ideas for her to try and encouraging her with prayer, as we slowly watched her marriage turn around.

God then opened several other doors for me to mentor women in their marriages that year. After one friend called to chat, I innocently asked, "How are you and your husband doing?" When she replied, "We're fine." I thought nothing of it, until five minutes later when she called back, choking back the tears and confiding that her marriage was a mess. For a year we met weekly, working through marriage books and emailing daily encouragements and prayers to each other. Praying out loud with another person still felt uncomfortable to me, yet how could we not bathe our time in prayer? Slowly, I saw Jesus refocus her from only seeing her husband's faults to working on her own brokenness.

At the same time, another friend usually called while steaming mad at her husband. Entering into someone else's strong emotions scared me to death and constantly reminded me how much I needed God. I listened, tried to refocus her on changes she could make, and reminded her of God's goodness and faithfulness. As I poured my life into these women, God started equipping me for my ministry.

Feeling burdened or responsible for other women's successes or failures could have easily paralyzed me. I remember sleepless nights filled with insecurity and worry. *What if I said the wrong thing? What if their husbands never changed?* I could listen to their stories and suggest different ways of thinking, but I couldn't *make* them do anything, nor could I guarantee that their husbands would respond the way they hoped. Finally, God conked me over the head and reminded me, "I am the one in control. You have to trust me. Just worship me!"

One of the passages that I still hang onto is 2 Corinthians 12:9-10: "But he said to me, 'My grace is sufficient for you, for my power is made perfect in weakness.' Therefore I will boast all the more gladly about my weaknesses, so that Christ's power may rest on me. That is why, for Christ's sake, I delight in weaknesses, in insults, in hardships, in persecutions, in difficulties. For when I am weak, then I am strong."

So many things that God has called me to do—praying over women, hearing their pain-filled stories, mentoring women, teaching sex classes, writing about sex, and speaking to groups—do not come naturally to me. I often feel like a fish out of water, yet I know that God has called me to this so I step out in obedience. Understanding that God is the One who changes lives, not me, has released me from expectations and pressures that would have given me the perfect excuse to avoid ministry.

God may call you to many changes in your sex life, none of which will come naturally. In order to grow, you will have to take risks and trust that God will work through even awkward blunders. You will even have to release control of your husband and trust God with him. Don't avoid change because it feels hard, expect to see God work.

I don't think I would have had the courage to mentor my friends or start teaching sex classes if not for my own mentor. Proverbs 27:17 says, "As iron sharpens iron, so one person sharpens another." Tiffany and I started meeting when I suggested we run together. Pretty soon she had us praising God through each letter of the alphabet to distract ourselves from the physical strain of running. I had no idea how profoundly she would shape my faith. Tiffany is one of those amazing women who prays on the spot and constantly asks God, "What do you want today?" I remember calling her in tears because I felt compelled to pray over other women. I was terrified and didn't have a clue how to start. Tiffany challenges me every day to live life fearlessly and to love God and serve others. God prepared me for ministry by opening doors to mentor women and by providing awesome mentors for me!

Transformation happens in community. You will need to process all you are learning with your husband and with friends. To get you started, discussion questions in each chapter will challenge you to open up conversations with your friends or husband. Processing our past with our husbands creates intimacy. Speaking our plans for growth gives us the courage to follow through. Sharing our testimonies of God's healing gives others hope. Transforming your sex life moves beyond your life when you start talking about sex.

## Teaching Sex Classes

After I started mentoring individual women in their marriages, I couldn't shake the feeling that God wanted me to address sex in our church. After gathering my courage, I marched into my pastor's office and exclaimed that our church needed to talk about sex. "All we ever hear from the church is 'don't do it!'" I told him. After he patiently listened to my concerns, we decided I would check out a sex conference at another church with Jim. Although many spiritual aspects of sex were addressed, questions concerning real applications remained unanswered.

Women need the whole story about sex—from the spiritual aspects, to how to deal with baggage, to how to talk about sex, to how to have an orgasm. I wanted to provide real answers to their questions. I finally realized that my pastor wasn't supposed to do something, *I was*. I knew that God was calling *me* to teach Christian sex classes to wives, and it terrified me.

A childhood experience created a deep-seated fear of public speaking. Even as a 40-year old, it didn't matter if it was a 10-second announcement or a class on sex, the thought of speaking in public was almost unbearable. *But how could I chicken out now? How could I not be obedient to my God that I so desperately loved?*

A few months later, Jim and I planned a winter get-away to relax for the weekend. At a secluded cabin we moved the futon mattress so we could overlook the frozen lake, and spent the entire weekend having sex, reading, talking, and having more sex. As I processed with Jim all that I had learned over the past year, the pieces began to fall into place. On the drive home, I sketched out on a scrap piece of paper the six-week curriculum for a class I'd call *Awaken-Love*. Two months later, I gathered up my nerve and sent an email to a dozen of my closest friends and asked them to be a part of the pilot class.

Eight of us met on my back porch. With the blessing of my pastor, I entered unchartered waters to help women find wholeness in their sexuality. I wanted to teach a class that pushed the envelope and challenged women's thinking while modeling open, respectful conversations. Our discussions ranged from wrestling with what sex teaches us about God to sharing fun creative ways to find freedom in our marriage bed.

The women came ready to learn and filled with grace for a teacher who had no idea what she was doing. I came with a rough outline of notes, good resources to share, and the sensitivity to create a safe place for conversation. I have no idea what I said those first classes and probably looked like a deer in the headlights. However, by week three, women lingered at the end of the evening to share how much the class had already affected them and their marriages.

Teaching was an act of obedience, a calling from God. I did not choose to teach. I felt compelled by God to do so. During each class, I was a nervous wreck; my lips would quiver and my mouth would be bone dry. Because I looked so uncomfortable speaking, friends constantly compared me to Moses. But the *Awaken-Love* class began to spread by word of mouth so I just kept teaching. Over and over again, women showed up, and over and over I got to watch God graciously work through my weaknesses so women could be changed. They came to class disillusioned, confused, and burdened, but they left feeling hopeful for the future and excited to share God's truth.

If God can use an ordinary woman like me who was terrified of public speaking and emotional vulnerability to start a grass roots movement about sex in church, then He can do anything.

I pray that my story will give you hope and courage to go after what God wants for you, and that your transformation will ripple and impact others to have a better understanding of God's powerful gift of sex.

## Action Items

1. Make a list of your fears about working on your sex life. Pray about them and give them to God.
2. Who do you have in your life that will speak truth over you and point you toward God as you process changes in your sex life? Start a conversation with a friend about the journey you are beginning.

# CHAPTER 3

# Finding Our Role

I DON'T HAVE A COLLEGE DEGREE IN SEXUALITY. I am just an ordinary woman who experienced a God-given ache for more intimacy and went looking for answers. After reading over a hundred books on sex from both Christian and secular perspectives, I've found as much bad information as good information. Put aside everything you've learned (or think you know), all of your assumptions about biblical marriage or what men and women need, and even past experiences from your own marriage. Start with a clean slate and go straight to the source: God's Word.

If we are looking for answers about sex in the Bible, we need to start with King Solomon's Song of Songs. It's no surprise that few sermons or studies are based on the Song of Songs; in fact, many women have told me "I didn't even know the book was in the Bible!" Song of Songs can both be interpreted as an allegory of God's love for us, the bride of Christ, but also as a manual for intimacy in marriage. The Song of Songs is unlike any other book in the Bible. It's an entire book full of explicit and descriptive poetry between two lovers, filled with imagery about sex. A young child reading it might think, "that's weird", but when we read the Song of Songs in class, women immediately think, "Oh my gosh, is *that* what they're talking about?"

Yep, if your mind goes there, that is where your mind is supposed to go! The Song of Songs is God's manual on marital intimacy. It is both detailed and spicy. Against all odds, this unique book made it into the Bible because God deemed it important to help us understand His amazing gift of sex.

Some women question how God can use Solomon to teach about intimacy when he had many wives and concubines. God often uses broken people. David, who committed adultery and murdered Bathsheba's husband, wrote most of the Psalms that teach us about having a heart for God. Moses, though afraid to speak, delivered the Israelites from slavery. God continues to use imperfect people, including me. Regardless of whether Song of Songs portrays Solomon's first love, I trust that God wants to teach us about intimacy in marriage through His Word.

The Song of Songs reads differently than any other book. Rather than speaking to our minds, it speaks to our hearts. Instead of giving us a set of rules, a list of the "dos and don'ts" for an intimate marriage, God paints a vivid portrait of a husband and wife intimately connecting with each other. We see them confront timeless struggles, such as a wife's insecurities about her beauty or a husband initiating sex at an inconvenient hour. In their responses to each other, we discover how they love each other with abandon. Rather than waiting for boredom to settle into their relationship, they constantly spur each other on, from the opening scene where she cries, "Kiss me and kiss me again", to the last line where she beckons, "Come away, my love!" They desire each other completely, embracing scents, tastes, sights, and sounds that reveal an intimacy in marriage that can feel almost like a fairy tale. Yet it's not a fairy tale; it is what God *wants* for your marriage!

One of the most surprising things about Song of Songs is the role the woman plays in their relationship. She talks as much as he does, expresses desires, communicates needs, daydreams about his body in explicate detail, and initiates an outdoor rendezvous in the vineyard. Contrast that to the role women played 3000 years ago when they had few rights. God is trying to tell us something! Regardless of women's role in culture, within the marriage bed, the wife should play an equal role. God intended that sex be as important to wives as it is to husbands.

*Discuss with your husband what roles you believed the husband and wife would play in the marriage bed.*

## Do It for You

Many women sign up for the Awaken-Love class because they know how important sex is for their husbands, but they have struggled to make it a priority. Though I confirm the ways sex positively affects their husbands, I encourage them to take the class for themselves. God created sex for them, too.

Wives pressured to take Awaken-Love by their husband or even a friend make little progress. They show up, reluctantly read, do minimal homework, and view everything through a lens of suspicion. With a hard heart, they do not hear or receive God's truth.

Wives looking for answers about sex come with open hearts and ready to learn. They understand the importance of sex for their husbands, but they quickly learn God has something for them, too. God's design resonates with their souls, and they quickly start recognizing lies they've believed about sex. Transformation of their mind comes in leaps and bounds as they embrace the simple truth that God created sex for them as much as their husbands. Walking out that truth requires intentionality, obedience, courage, and faith as they embrace freedom in the marriage bed.

This is not unlike our faith. At some point, our faith must become our own. If our parents or friends force us to attend church, resentment builds and our hearts become hard. Others cannot make us fall in love with Jesus. Until we decide we want a personal relationship with Christ, we just check church off the to-do list. But when we desperately cry out, "I need Jesus," God does a work in us. Transformation and understanding can come in an instant but walking out our faith takes a lifetime. We still have to intentionally spend time with God, take steps of growth through obedience, and continue to learn more about Him. Our faith is a journey and only *we* can decide if we want to take that journey. The same is true about intimacy in marriage.

Many wives think they have sex figured out. They understand the importance of sex for their husbands, make it a priority, and even enjoy sex themselves. As they begin to study Song of Songs, they realize that all of these years they've really been having sex for their husband. When they realize God created sex for them too and that they have something to offer, they can embrace the freedom God wants for them. Song of Songs tells us that God intended sex to be as important to wives as it is to husbands. We should be mutual partners in the marriage bed —equal but different.

## Equal but Different

The more I learn about sex, the more I understand God's powerful design to refine both husband and wife through marriage. He created man and woman—*both* in His image, but so very different from each other. As we work towards creating an intimate sex life, we stretch to meet each other's needs and learn from one another.

Many women question why God made sex so complicated for us and so easy for our husbands. We can feel broken or defective. But if sex were easy for both of us, it wouldn't create intimacy. Vulnerably sharing our needs, praying over baggage, and showing our husband what works all create intimacy. Having hard conversations, understanding each other's insecurities, and extending grace to each other create intimacy. If sex were as hard for husbands as it is for wives, both parties would probably just give up.

Women might feel like they got the shorter end of the stick but imagine how a loving husband feels. His greatest desire is to give pleasure to his wife. Can you imagine how frustrated and confused he feels as he tries to figure out his very complicated wife? Sex is hard for both of us.

Sex stretches us toward personal growth. Creating a sex life that wives enjoy will require us to express our desire and tap into our God-given creativity. We must learn to use our words to create arousal and teach our husbands to do the same. We will have to communicate and demonstrate how to move from routines to being present with each other.

Even though the mechanics of sex and orgasm come easily to our husbands, intimacy may not. Moving beyond movement and creating arousal through connection can feel foreign and even scary to a husband. Looking into each other's eyes, feeling each other's bodies through stillness, and speaking words of excitement challenge a husband to stretch to meet his wife's needs. Along the way, he discovers a connection sweeter than anything he ever imagined.

We have something to bring to the table: creating a sex life that *we* look forward to will cause our husbands to grow! Contrary to what we have been raised to believe, we are not just supposed to have sex for the sake of our husbands. Unless we embrace our role as equals, our husbands will miss out on experiencing what only we can show them.

**With your husband, brainstorm ways the two of you are different when it comes to sex and affirm each other's differences.**

## Final Thoughts

Over and over I watch women experience profound growth when they embrace the truth that God created sex for them too. Rather than aim for just a short-term fix of prioritizing sex for their husbands, their whole mindset changes. They begin to believe God created sex to not only strengthen their marriage but also as an intimate way to know their husbands. They dare to believe that sex can provide comfort and restoration, not only for their husbands but for them, too. Rather than just going along for the ride, they help create new experiences.

When I realized the importance of sex for me, I became a mutual partner invested in creating intimate connection. After letting go of defining my sexuality by how Jim operated, I embraced our differences. I showed Jim how to connect with words to make sex an adventure. He taught me how to be more spontaneous and let go of the worries of the day. We slowed things down and focused more on the journey than the destination. Together we learned to experience intimate communion. Embracing God's design of mutuality in the marriage bed was the first step of believing the truth about sex.

## Action Items

1. Read Song of Songs and think about the role the woman (the "beloved") plays versus the role that he (the "lover") plays.
2. What are ways that you have received the message, "Do it for your husband"?

# CHAPTER 4

# Oneness

I USED TO THINK MY HUSBAND reached for me just because he needed a sexual release—like an itch that needed to be scratched or an animal on the prowl for his next meal. I assumed the testosterone coursing through his body controlled him regardless of life circumstances. Every nice thing my husband did caused me to pause and question if his hidden desires motivated his actions. I bought into the cultural message that men don't care about love, intimacy, or connection. They just need sex.

Many of you may relate. We get irritated when our husbands reach for us and we're not in the mood. *Can't he see that I am tired or that I have a lot on my mind? Can't he just control himself? He needs to learn to love me in other ways. How can he even think about sex at a time like this?* Accusations about our husbands fill our heads.

But the reality of sex in my marriage was different than I thought. As a happily-married couple, my husband and I had a good sex life. We'd figured out what worked, and we enjoyed making love. But honestly, we had gotten to the place where we only had sex when I felt interested. You know, those twice a month hormonal spikes, usually near ovulation and just before your period? I had become the gatekeeper and those were pretty much the only times we'd have sex.

So . . . who in our marriage thought sex was only physical? I only allowed us to have sex when *my* hormones spiked, when *I* felt horny.

Had I bought into the cultural messages that sex was just about satisfying my own personal needs, no different than eating, drinking, and sleeping? Was it possible that we were missing out on a powerful way to connect that went far beyond urges and hormones? Did my husband intuitively understand something that I did not?

## God's Design

God created sex to make two into one. Genesis 2:24 says, "That is why a man leaves his father and mother and is united to his wife, and they become one flesh." God unites a man and a woman through marriage. He takes two completely different people and joins them into one—emotionally, spiritually, and physically. He intertwines their lives like a vine tangled around itself. When one spouse hurts, the other hurts. When one feels excited, the other feels energized. The happiness of a wife becomes integrally connected to the happiness of her husband.

One of the ways God makes us into one is through the physical act of sex. One body joins to another, vulnerably opening up and experiencing pleasure. Even science supports the bonding that takes place due to the release of powerful chemicals like oxytocin in the brain during lovemaking. Having sex unites husband and wife and has been a foundational part of the marriage relationship since its inception.

Engaging in this act together does something to our marriages and to us in the process. It glues us together so that we can survive the bumps and bruises of living in a fallen world. Though church rarely talks about the importance of sex to create oneness *in* marriage, we often hear about it *outside* of marriage.

If you grew up in the church, you might remember purity messages from youth group when your pastor used some crazy illustration for sex outside of marriage:

"This red piece of construction paper represents you," he'd say, "and the green paper represents your boyfriend." He'd then proceed to squirt glue onto the pieces of paper and press them together. "This glue represents you two having sex." Then after talking about all of the dangers of sex outside of marriage, he'd slowly peel the papers apart. Glue had caused part of the red paper to tear off, forever stuck to the green–a stark reminder that when you have sex, you give part of yourself to your partner. And when that relationship is temporary, you leave part of yourself behind forever when you walk away.

This metaphor holds true for sex *in* marriage as well. Sex *is* like glue. It sticks two people together and creates oneness. Even though the message is drilled into us as teenagers, it doesn't get the same emphasis in marriage, and women seem to forget about it.

*Discuss with your friends the idea of Oneness and share examples of when sex helped glue your marriages together.*

## Men Understand Oneness

Have you ever experienced your husband wanting to have sex even when you were in the midst of an unresolved disagreement? I remember days when my husband and I just could not get on the same page. Eventually we would decide to just go to bed and address the problem in the morning. As I tossed and turned still pouting in bed, my husband would gently reach for me and I would just reel back. "You've got to be kidding. How can you think about sex now? We haven't worked this out yet!"

I felt hurt, angry, and even confused that my loving husband could even think about sex now. I've since realized that when my husband reached for me, he didn't just need a physical release. He reached for me because he somehow intuitively understood the power of oneness. He didn't know what to say or what to do to make things better. Jim didn't even know how to explain it. All he knew was that if we could make love, God would help us get on the same page. Sex would glue us back together.

After talking to hundreds of men and women, I believe most men intuitively understand the power of oneness from sex while wives have much to learn. Instead, we constantly agree with marriage books that write, "Women need to be emotionally connected to their husbands in order to have sex, and men need to have sex in order to emotionally connect to their wives."

On the surface, this statement totally makes sense. When my husband and I connect through intimate conversations or spending time laughing or being together, I feel close to him. It gets me in the mood when he wants to hear how I feel or when he shares from his heart. Connecting first emotionally comes naturally to me, and most women agree.

Men, on the other hand, seem to work in the opposite direction. The average man has a hard time connecting with his wife emotionally if she has shut him out sexually. Men tend to withdraw out of rejection, bury themselves in work, or tune out in front of a screen when they feel sexually rejected. But after a husband enjoys great sex with his wife, he naturally opens up to her.

These may be our natural tendencies, but that does not mean God wants us to stay there. When both husband and wife insist on what feels natural and easy, their marriage spins further and further towards disconnection. We resort to bartering, "If you talk to me, then we can have sex." Or, "If you have sex, then I can talk to you!"

Men have plenty of room to grow. They *do* need to learn to talk to us and share their feelings, whether or not we have connected physically.

But *we* also have something to learn! We must remember that God mysteriously creates oneness in marriage every single time we have sex. Making love will help us to be more open to each other, to hear and understand each other better. Sex communicates things when words fall short. When we cannot agree, maybe what we need most is to have sex with our husbands.

During class Bonnie shared, "The other night my husband and I were in the middle of a situation. And just like you said, he initiated sex. In the past, I probably would have pushed him away. But because of what we've talked about I decided to try something different. I prayed and asked God to help me really engage. Afterwards, we still had to work through our problem, but somehow it seemed easier. Having sex helped us to understand each other."

Nothing that Bonnie did was easy. Opening yourself up, dropping your defenses, and willingly becoming naked and vulnerable when you're disconnected from your husband does not come naturally. It takes trusting that your husband does not just need a physical release, but that he loves you and desires to reconnect with you. It takes trusting God and asking for help: "God, help me to let go of the need to control, and to trust you. Help my body to respond to my husband's touch and help me enter into this with my whole heart."

Stepping into what does not come naturally matures us and drives us towards a dependence on God. It causes us to pause and say, "Help me, God! I can't do this on my own."

*Ask your husband why he has initiated sex when you are in disagreement.*

## Be Interruptible

God portrays a situation many women relate to in Song of Songs 5:2-3 when the Beloved says, "I slept but my heart was awake. Listen! My beloved is knocking." In the middle of the night the Lover implores her, "Open to me, my sister, my darling, my dove, my flawless one. My head is drenched with dew, my hair with dampness of the night." And she replies the way that most of us would when our husbands approach us at inconvenient times, "I have taken off my robe—must I put it on again? I have washed my feet—must I soil them again?" In other words, "Are you kidding? Now?"

This timeless challenge in Song of Songs portrays a husband initiating when his wife feels less than enthusiastic. A husband needs to pay attention to his wife's needs and learn to initiate at good times. But there is also something for *us* to learn.

My mentor Tiffany constantly prays, "God, help me to be interruptible." Even in the midst of a busy day with her agenda full of important tasks, she puts God first. If He calls her to take a moment to pray over a friend, help a single mom with childcare, or just sit still with Him, she makes time. She doesn't want to ever have her day so set in stone that she misses out on what God has for her.

The same applies in marriage. If we control everything about our lives, we might miss out on what our husbands have for us. Is it possible that some of those inconvenient times your husband reaches for you are when he really needs to feel your love? Could entering into oneness lead to amazing memories and help us learn how to let go of control? Can we allow our lives to be interruptible, with God and even with our husbands?

## Oneness Beyond Sex

Sometimes we might not even realize the impact oneness can create in marriage. During a discussion about creating intimacy by praying together as husband and wife, Kati, one of my students shared, "I cannot even imagine praying together with my husband. He'll hardly even go to church, much less pray with me." Even though discouraged, she stuck with the class and committed to love and minister to her husband through sex.

A couple of weeks later, Kati's husband was happily sitting with her at church. Pretty soon they were showing up at church marriage events. A few months later, the impossible happened and he signed up to go on a mission trip to Africa. Along the road to oneness with his wife, Kati's husband opened up to Jesus. God used their sexual relationship to soften him and to reach him, and to make him into one with her.

Since then, this gentle, reserved husband has quietly acknowledged the impact of his wife's sexual transformation on his life. It affected not only his marriage, but his relationship with God.

Sex makes you into one—not just on your wedding night, but every single time you make love. It makes you into one by fitting your bodies together, but it unites the two of you in more than just the physical sense. Sex makes you into one physically, emotionally, and even spiritually.

Everything in this world tries to tear your marriage apart—kids, work, screens, your own selfishness—and you need sex to keep putting the two of you back together. Sex gets you back on the same page and clears out all of the junk that tries to divide you. God uses sex to bring the two of you together in ways that you cannot do yourself.

## Final Thoughts

Tapping into the power of sex to make us into one has challenged me to wrestle with what I believe about my husband and what I believe about sex. Do I trust that when my husband reaches for me, he doesn't just need a physical release? Are there times when my husband realizes that we need to connect, and I'm oblivious? Is sex more than just physical pleasure driven by hormones? If God created sex as a way to connect us and love each other, why should I wait to have sex until I am already feeling connected to my husband? Maybe sometimes I just need to trust God.

I have discovered the power of sex to make my husband and me into one. Whether or not my body desires sex, I know that we need to come together so that God can unite us. The more we come together as one, the more He glues us together.

## Action

1. Try having sex when you don't feel emotionally connected to your husband. Don't just go through the motions but try to get on board. Notice what it does to your relationship.

2. Pray about what it would look like for you to be interruptible – to God and to your husband.

# CHAPTER 5

# Being Known

MY HUSBAND AND I are both pretty even-keeled engineers—rational, practical, and safe. We grew up in Christian
families that gathered around the dinner table to discuss the
latest news. Together we build decks, remodel kitchens, and
replace furnaces. Some people might say we had an ideal marriage, but in many ways, we had a "safe" marriage. We didn't
talk about hard things. We didn't talk about God or pray together. We definitely didn't talk about sex.

Early on, Jim and I figured out what worked for us in our
marriage bed and we just stuck with it. Sex wasn't bad, but at
times I felt frustrated or maybe even bored. I knew we were
missing out on something, but I didn't know what. Some
nights I resorted to fantasizing in order to create the boost my
body needed to finish.

Year in and year out, we had sex the same way, because
just like most Christians, we felt uncomfortable discussing

sex. Changing things would have required sharing our desires, and neither one of us had the nerve to do that.

One of the reasons God created sex was to "know" each other. Genesis 4:1 says, "And Adam knew his wife Eve, and she conceived and bare Cain..." (KJV).

God created sex for us to know each other—physically, emotionally and spiritually—and yet a lot of us are *not* getting to know each other.

## Challenges to Knowing

Getting to know each other through sex is not easy. People who have sex in noncommitted relationships can be much freer in their sexuality. They hold nothing back and just go for it because they are not vested in that relationship. But when we get married, all of a sudden, we wake up next to the most important person in the world to us. *What would he think if I showed him that part of me? What if he didn't like it? What if he laughed?* We get married and we limit ourselves. We put ourselves in this safe box and have safe sex. Then we wonder how sex got so boring.

Silence surrounds sex in the church, and so many of us connect sex with shame. Even though we know God created sex for marriage, we struggle to step into real freedom because we separate God from sex. We close our bedroom doors and leave God on the other side. We are certain He doesn't want to know what is going on in here. So we continue having sex in the same old way, masked in silence and escaping to our own worlds. Rather than discovering new things or enjoying the journey, we focus on the finish line. Worrying about performance causes us to observe sex instead of experience sex. Our discomfort talking about sex creates huge barriers to knowing each other, leaving many of us with pretty mediocre sex lives and missing out on the blessings God has for us.

"Getting to know each other" is the key to *how* we have sex. It will revolutionize your marriage bed. Instead of bringing things from the outside in to make sex exciting, you simply bring yourself. With fresh eyes, you explore and discover as God grants you freedom to creatively share yourself. You will learn to make love not just in a variety of ways but with a depth that sees into each other's souls. Sex will get better and better as you learn to read each other's bodies and anticipate ways to love each other. When you get to know each other, sex never gets boring; it gets sweeter and sweeter.

## Women Crave "Knowing"

In the same way that men tune into "oneness," women tune into "knowing" during sex. "Knowing" will determine whether women love sex or could care less. Most women can relate to this scenario:

You finally warm up to the idea of sex and relax into letting things happen. A little kiss here, a little touch there, and then suddenly you recognize what he's doing. He's started his routine. You know exactly where he's going next, and you can't stop your brain from thinking, *Here we go again. Yep, here we go again.*

You don't say anything for fear of ruining the mood, but you continue becoming more and more agitated. Your body gets tense with your mind clicking, *Yep, same thing again. Really? Does he even notice that I'm not enjoying this?*

Now your husband may be so intent on getting you to the finish line that he truly doesn't notice. He forges on, determined to make it work because it worked last time. Meanwhile, you continue getting more and more tense and frustrated.

But if he actually notices that you are not enjoying it, or if he feels the tension in your body, he will stop. He will think to himself, *Maybe I should try another path.*

Suddenly we are back on board. *He actually noticed that I wasn't enjoying it. He is paying attention to me. He's getting to know me.*

God created women in tune to His design of "knowing" each other. We challenge our husbands to learn to intimately connect during sex rather than just go through their routine. We sense when they pay attention or when they fill with anxiety or worry. Going through the motions turns us off, while his fascination and discovery thrill us. We want our husbands to study and understand every detail of our minds and bodies and souls—and we have plenty to understand. But we cannot expect our husbands to figure us out on their own. We have to communicate, express ourselves and encourage them in the small steps that they take. We have to help them to know us.

## Variety and Depth

"Knowing" happens in two directions. The horizontal axis represents variety. Different positions, different types of stimulation, and different locations can help us discover what arouses and brings us pleasure. The vertical axis represents a depth of knowing. It grows with studying each other and feels like a well-worn pair of slippers that brings a smile to our faces.

The horizontal axis contains the intentional choices that we make to expand our repertoire by learning to enjoy intercourse, manual stimulation, oral sex, or some other delight. You can create variations by showing your husband how to stimulate you in a whole array of positions—face-to-face, spooning, sitting between his legs, face-to-your-body, or you straddling him. All of these positions feel very different, even though they all involve manual stimulation. The different positions hold a different energy and convey a different mood. Together you explore different locations or outfits and how they make you feel. You also begin to understand the comfort of "meat and potatoes" sex in your favorite position. You don't just expand your repertoire for variety's sake. You fill your tool belt so that you can fully express yourself during sex.

The vertical axis is a "knowing of the soul" that goes beyond words or actions and does not come naturally in our busy, performance-based culture. It is like when you meet with God and you have your own agenda. You read your scripture for the day and pray through your requests, and all the while God is yelling, "Hey, can you hear me? I'm here. Stop. Listen to me. Just come and be with me and discover something new about who I am. "

In our busy, goal-oriented world, "knowing" God does not come easily; it takes letting go of both control and expectations. We have to listen and ask questions. Rather than hanging onto our own agenda, we must allow God to interrupt us and sometimes just sit in His presence. We have to ask Him to show us who He is so that we can recognize His voice. As we encounter His glory, we should fill with awe as we simply praise Him.

In the same way, knowing each other in depth during sex is less about mechanics and more about connection. We learn to move together without thinking because we tune into each other's bodies. We speak truth and reassurance because we know the hurts and insecurities that come from wounds of the past. Eye to eye, gentle smiles acknowledge a presence of entering together into the Holy of Holies. Performance, anxiety, and expectations are exchanged for discovery, being, and openness.

In essence then, the horizontal axis starts by you expanding ways to express yourself in a language needed to understand each other. The vertical axis gradually comes into play as you focus on connection and create depth—a knowing of the soul that goes beyond words or actions.

It is like learning to dance. You start with the basic steps of 1-2-3 for the Fox Trot, and you practice until you no longer have to count in your head. Then you add variations like spins and dips. As you add more and more dance moves, with practice you get comfortable with each other. Eventually you think about the actual steps less and less and just get lost in the music. Eventually you learn some other dances like the Waltz or the Lindy that go with different moods and types of music. Then you have this whole repertoire of dances that allow you to just move together instead of thinking about the actual steps. You start to read each other and freely transition from one dance to the other based on the music and what you feel like. Eventually you don't even know who is leading; the two of you simply move together.

Our world is filled with distractions that keep us from knowing our spouses. Screens grab our gaze and prevent us from spending time captivated eye to eye. The rush of schedules leaves little time to linger long enough to catch the aroma of our lover. "Being" gets replaced with "to do" lists. We simply co-exist in parallel lives. But God knew that it would take men and women a long time to figure one another out. That's why he didn't say "stay together for a year"; he told us to stay together for a lifetime.

We must create time to know each other—and what better place than the marriage bed? We cannot read a spouse's mind, but we can learn to read a spouse's body. One of the most important physical techniques for reading a spouse's body is the concept of rubbing vs. feeling. Try the exercise as you read along.

*Talk with your husband about what keeps you from getting to know each other. Brainstorm solutions together.*

## Rubbing vs. Feeling

Take your right hand and spend about 30 seconds rubbing your left wrist. Stop. Then do it again. Only this time instead of rubbing, I want you to feel your wrist. Spend time focusing on feeling the surface of the skin. Then try to feel underneath the skin by taking your time to follow the paths of the tendons or the veins. Feel across them and feel their strength. Next completely eliminate friction by keeping your fingers attached to the skin on your wrist. Slowly try to feel as much detail as you can underneath the skin. You might even hold your hand still and see if you can pick up a pulse.

*What changed when you went from rubbing to feeling?*

Besides the obvious answer of a dramatic reduction in speed, *feeling* involved your mind. You paid attention to what you felt. You took the information from your fingertips up into your brain and made a mental map, or a memory. With focused time and practice, you would begin to recognize when your wrist felt tense or relaxed. Instead of mindlessly rubbing your wrist, you got to "know" it.

Trust me, women know the difference between rubbing and feeling. We do not want our husbands to rub us in order to get from point A to B. Our greatest desire is that our husbands get to know us. We want them to feel us, study our body, try new things, know when our body relaxes or tenses, and learn to take us on amazing journeys.

## Letting Yourself Be Known

Knowing is a two-way street. If you want your spouse to know you through sex, then you have to let yourself be known. You could lie there stiff as a board, completely silent, and frustrate even the most committed loving husband. You have to let your body respond to what it enjoys. You have to communicate and express your desires, but you also have to vulnerably share past experiences that have shaped you. Sex is not just a means for your husband to know you physically, but a way for him to know you emotionally and spiritually as well—even your sexual baggage.

When Sharmane signed up for class, she came seeking intimacy more than sexual techniques. Years of hard work and raising not only her own kids, but her grandkids, nephews, and step-kids had taken its toll on Sharmane's looks. You might not guess now, but Sharmane used to be stunning and confessed to working in a strip club in her youth. As Sharmane received love, grace, and acceptance from other women in class, she gained courage to open up to her husband. Nervous but determined to be known, she eventually sat him down to share about the hurt and abuse she had suffered from countless men. Careful not to share specific details that might create pain for her husband, she talked about feeling used as men interested only in their own gratification ogled her in the club. For weeks afterward, Sharmane spoke of how tenderly her husband treated her ever since their talk. Because of her courage, he knew her in a new way.

Sharing our baggage creates intimacy. It encourages appreciation for our struggles and compassion as we grow, whether that means sharing our first experiences of learning about sex, painful memories of being used, or falling into porn. If we want to know each other 100%, then we must have the courage to be known —not to hurt our spouse with painful vivid details, but to share in general ways how our past has impacted us.

## Expressing Ourselves During Sex

When you get to know each other through sex, then sex becomes this amazing way to represent who you are at that moment in time. Sex looks different based on how you feel.

For instance, if you feel insecure, you might want your husband to cover your body and to press you between the bed with his strength. Quick movements or sudden loss of contact make you feel as if you just fell off a cliff, while connected movements hold you secure.

When you are in a playful mood, you might be game for any position. You can tease each other and surprise each other as you give and take the lead. Your eyes watch wide open, anticipating his next move and enjoying the show of your bodies joining together.

When you feel gutsy and confident, then you are ready to fully expose yourself as you take charge. You enjoy your husband's eyes on you and give him a show. You move like you want to move, you put his hands where you want them, and you make sure that he knows without a doubt that you are in charge.

When you are feeling sensuous, you move so slowly that he can feel every fiber of your being. You stretch your body taut as the tension builds. When you are in tune to stillness, you feel the smallest intention that can lead to a ripple of goodness. You focus on more subtle connections, like the sound of your husband's breath or the smells you create.

Over the years of getting to know each other, gaining confidence, and expanding your repertoire, sex can represent the way you feel, but it takes communication, intentionality, and *lots* of practice. You have to express the kind of sex you want in certain moods, how he should hold you, and even come up with phrases to key him into how you feel. Sex should not always look the same; it should express how you feel at that moment in time.

Our decision to let ourselves be fully known must be grounded in the reality that God created us exactly like He wanted us. Ephesians 2:10 says, "For we are God's handiwork, created in Christ Jesus to do good works, which God prepared in advance for us to do." God loves every detail of us, and in marriage He will give us the strength to be fully known. He wants to give us a little taste of the Garden of Eden during sex, to be naked and unashamed. Dive in and hang on tight to God.

*With your husband, brainstorm what confident sex, playful sex, or comfort sex might look like for you.*

## Final Thoughts

Sex for me and my husband has dramatically changed since we have tuned into getting to know each other during sex. We no longer focus on the end goal but on what we can discover. Gentle smiles pass back and forth as we acknowledge our presence. Words pull us back toward each other, affirm each other, and guide our path. Some of the sweetest moments are the unfiltered reactions and yearnings expressed in the heat of the moment. I can feel my husband's movements and join him, or he can join mine. Rather than worry or observe, we just are.

But don't think for a second that my husband and I have this all figured out. I still slip back into worrying about having an orgasm or letting expectations affect what I enjoy. Letting my husband know me has been one of the hardest things I have ever done. I have vulnerably gotten naked over and over again. Sharing my insecurities over beauty and asking for his words of affirmation laid me bare. Stepping things up a notch to create what I found exciting was terrifying. Praying about my sexual baggage exposed some of the most sensitive parts of my soul. Allowing my body to freely respond and express itself took enormous trust. But I love it when my husband slyly shares after sex, "I learned something new about you tonight," with a sparkle in his eye like a kid who just found a new toy.

God calls us to be known. It is not easy, but I cannot imagine anything else.

## Action Items

1. Choose one sense (taste, touch, smell, etc.) to focus on in order to be more present during sex.
2. Have sex with your eyes open.

# CHAPTER 6

# Refreshment
# and Comfort

SEVERAL TIMES A YEAR, moms groups invite me to speak about sex. As I scan the room filled with tired moms bouncing babies on their laps, I often think, *Great, just what these mommas need. One more thing to do.*

And I have to catch myself, because that was my old mindset.

Years ago, I remember trying to get dinner on the table with four young girls swirling around my legs. Worn thin by parenting, while my husband was at the office, I felt like he was on the opposite team. By the time he got home, I could have had daggers coming out of my eyes when he tried to cozy up to me.

Other times when I got involved in a big project and felt stressed, I would literally stiff-arm Jim if he reached for me.

"Just let me figure this out; then we can connect." I wanted nothing to do with sex until I had my life put together. Only then could I relax with my husband.

For most women, sex feels like one more thing on our "to do" lists. Whether we spend all day changing diapers or climbing the corporate ladder, sex is often the last thing on our minds. It seems like one more obligation that will drain the life out of us. As exhausted women, we think, "Surely I should have a break from *that*. Doesn't anyone understand how tired I am?"

But God never meant for sex to suck the life out of us. In fact, God intended quite the opposite! God wants to refresh us, to fill us up, and to even comfort us through intimate connection with our husbands. What if sex could help you and your husband thrive in the midst of the day-to-day battles of raising kids? What if sex could act as a refuge from the chaos or the hard things you and your husband face? What if sex could even comfort you in the midst of grief?

## Refreshment

In Proverbs 5:15-18, Solomon writes a warning against adultery:

> Drink water from your own cistern,
>    running water from your own well.
> Should your springs overflow in the streets,
>    your streams of water in the public squares?
> Let them be yours alone,
>    never to be shared with strangers
> May your fountain be blessed,
>    and may you rejoice in the wife of your youth.

Among the most striking parts of this passage are the metaphors used to represent sex. We read of running water and springs that refresh and quench our thirst. We see streams and fountains that mesmerize and bring newness of life. God intended sex to refresh us, both individually and as a couple. His design was to provide satisfaction and continued intrigue as we discover each other through sex. God wants sex to be a fountain that we return to over and over when our life feels barren and dry.

In Song of Songs 1:2, the Beloved says, "Let him kiss me with the kisses of his mouth – for your love is more delightful than wine."

Think about what a glass of wine does after a long day. You finally get the kids in bed, wash the last dish piled in the sink, and plunk down on the couch. Your husband brings you a small glass of wine. Just a small sip and, AHHH . . . the stress of the day begins to melt away.

God intended kissing, physical connection, and even SEX to help us relax and reconnect. He made it so sex would relieve the tension in our bodies, melt away our worries, and refresh us. He designed sex to help us even more than a glass of wine at the end of the day, and science can back that up too!

Scientists have confirmed that sex reduces stress, lowers blood pressure, improves sleep, and decreases headaches. Sex can physically help our bodies handle life.

Just taking that minute to greet your spouse after work can help refresh both of you. Ignoring the chaos for a moment and making time to kiss or hug each other can help you both physically relax. This connection puts you on the same page,

and afterwards, it lets you both know that you can do this—
*together*.

It is no different than my relationship with God. When I
am busy and stressed, I have a hard time remembering to
make time to really sit with God. I am too busy trying to handle life on my own. I have to remind myself of what my
friend Jessie says: "Ruth, you need to get with God." I need to
just sit still with God. I need to cry out to Him and ask for
help. I need to pray and commune with Him and release my
worries to Him.

Sometimes my husband knows just what I need, even
when I don't. Gently he approaches me to offer a backrub
with no expectations. Sometimes I relax and slowly open up
to enjoy a sexual encounter. And afterwards I often think to
myself, *Man, did I need that!* Sex just wiped my slate clean. It
released every last bit of tension that made me snippy and
impatient. After sex, my mind feels clearer and life less daunt-
ing.

Many of us think our husbands offer backrubs simply to
trick us into having sex. What if that isn't the case at all?
What if our husbands genuinely understand how much sex
would help to ease our tension? Maybe we don't need to have
everything under control in order to enter into sex.

It is the same idea as thinking that we need to have our
lives put together before we come to God. When we're a
mess, when we're not in the Word, or when we feel distant,
we avoid church and we stiff-arm God. We avoid our Christian friends, thinking we need to get our lives together first.
God wants us to come to Him even in our mess, even when
we are broken and needy. He wants us to stop trying to fix

everything or control things. We need to trust Him, surrender, and just come to him.

Matthew 11:28 says, "Come to me, all you who are weary and burdened, and I will give you rest." What if you decided to trust God on this? Could you ask Him to help you get on board with connecting with your husband, even when it's not at the forefront of your mind? Maybe through learning how to let go to enjoy sex, we understand a little more about how to let go so that we can get lost with God. What if you decided to just give it a try and see what happens?

Those times when life seems crazy and sex is the last thing on your mind might be the time when you need sex the most! Whether we are in the season of caring for babies, carting kids to soccer, or working on an intense project at work, focused time together can unite us and make us into one. It can also refresh us. By turning off the phones and the computer, we can escape and just go be together. We stop thinking about the schedule or the worries and just get lost in each other.

*With some girlfriends, talk about whether sex feels like refreshment. Wrestle with why or why not.*

## Comfort

God also created sex to comfort us. When David and Bathsheba lost their child, it says in 2 Samuel 12:24, "Then David comforted his wife Bathsheba, and he went to her and made love to her." God intended for sex to comfort us, even during the loss of a child.

When we think about sex as a comfort, we usually think about times we might comfort our husbands after a rough day at work, during a job loss, or in the midst of a personal loss.

Many women have shared about comforting their husbands through sex and how much it helped.

Interestingly, this passage talks about David comforting Bathsheba, not Bathsheba comforting David. God created sex as a way for husbands to comfort wives. For many of us, this idea requires a real leap of faith.

Most of us grew up without positive messages about sex. We went from strong purity messages of "don't do it" to messages of "do it for your husband." If sex feels like a duty, it should come as no surprise that few of us understand the power of sex to refresh, restore, or comfort.

In one of my classes, a woman shared that after she lost her mother, her husband initiated sex. She couldn't believe it! How could he think about sex right now, of all times? As I discussed this further with her, tears filled her eyes as she realized that her husband hadn't been acting like some inconsiderate jerk. He just wanted to comfort her in the only way he knew how—by intimately connecting with her skin to skin.

I have also talked to women who have experienced sex as an amazing source of comfort during really painful situations. After losing her brother to cancer, Shelly went to her husband and said, "Can we just have sad sex?" She needed him to enter into her grief as they made love to each other. Another woman, Katie, shared, that when there were no words left after grieving the loss of their baby, she and her husband found comfort in each other's arms.

Sex spoke things that words could not and held them together. Through physical intimacy, women were able to use painful situations to glue themselves to their husbands instead of pull them apart. Women who have experienced sex as a comfort timidly share with a sincerity and tenderness that almost feels supernatural. God meets them in their grief as they commune with their husbands.

*Ask your husband if he has ever experienced sex as a comfort and when.*

## Serving Each Other

God's view of sex is in stark contrast with the world's view. God's plan is not about taking what you can, but about serving and loving each other. His amazing gift helps us to refresh and comfort each other. In Song of Songs 1:13-14, the woman says,

> My beloved is to me a sachet of myrrh
> resting between my breasts.
> My beloved is to me a cluster of henna blossoms
> from the vineyards of En Gedi.

A sachet of myrrh (a small pouch of perfume) rests between her breasts to remind her of her lover. His aroma causes her to long for him all day. He is like a cluster of henna blossoms from En Gedi, an oasis in the middle of a rocky dessert.

A woman shared how Awaken-Love changed her marriage. She said, "My husband and I have a strong marriage and we've always had a good sex life. What impacted me most about the class was the idea of sex being a comfort. It was not something I had ever considered or related to. One night I came home from an awful day at work, completely discouraged." With tears in her eyes she said, "I would never have done this in the past, but I reached for my husband. I reached for my husband for comfort, and God met us there. What an amazing, sweet thing."

To me, her tears said it all. She discovered a depth of intimacy with her husband beyond physical connection that touched her soul. Don't relegate sex to physical pleasure. God wants sex to refresh you and comfort your heavy heart.

God gave us marriage and intimate connection as an oasis to escape to when life gets hard. God never intended for sex to become a "to do" list to drain our energy. He wants sex to fill us up, refresh us, and even comfort us.

## Final Thoughts

I remember the first time I experienced sex as a comfort. I had just started teaching Awaken-Love, and even though classes went great, I would wake up in the middle of the night wracked with insecurities. Voices in my head swirled, *"Who do you think you are? What do you know about sex? This isn't really making a difference."* My husband and I finally decided that on nights when I taught class, we needed to make love. Sex communicated my husband's support and belief in me. Sex comforted me in the midst of my insecurities—plus, sex provided great sleep!

Sex has drastically changed for me, and I find myself reaching for my husband at times I never would have before. When I feel sad because of struggles friends face in their marriage, sex comforts me. When I feel unsure of myself or overwhelmed by life, my husband comforts me. When I feel myself slipping towards depression, making love helps to pull me out of the pit. Connecting with my husband fills me up and refreshes me. It strengthens me to do what God has called me to do.

Sex does not take the place of God, and neither does my husband. Above all else, I have to spend time getting filled up, restored, and comforted by God. But God gave me my husband, a godly man, to physically hold on to; a man who can speak words of life and truth to me. God gave us sex as a way to love each other and communicate things that words cannot. Finding restoration in sex shows me what a good God I serve.

## Action Items

1. Pray about why sex does not feel like refreshment. What lies have you believed?
2. Practice finding refreshment through physical connection. Greet your husband every day this week with a 15-second kiss.

# CHAPTER 7

# A Picture of Intimacy

As I have wrestled with what God wants for my sex life, I've spent a lot of time reading Christian marriage and sex books in search of answers. One of my toughest challenges has been discerning what is true about sex and what is not. So many things I read about sex felt wrong, but I struggled at first with how to biblically test them. Finally, God pointed me to Ephesians 5:31-32: which says, "'For this reason a man will leave his father and mother and be united to his wife, and the two will become one flesh.' This is a profound mystery—but I am talking about Christ and the church."

**Becoming one is a picture of intimacy with Christ.**

***Sex* is a picture of intimacy with Christ.**

When we want to figure out God's intention for sex in marriage, we measure it against the intimacy that Christ wants to have with us. We understand the importance of the heart versus just going through the motions during sex. Learning to surrender our worries to God helps us learn how to let go of control so we can make love. Sex becomes more about meeting with each other than about results. This principle of Ephesians will uproot every lie the world has told us about sex and will help us sort out what comes naturally from what God desires.

## Measuring God's Intention for Sex

Let me give you a couple of examples of how we can use intimacy with Christ to measure God's truth about sex.

The world tells us that monogamous sex within marriage will become boring. Time together strips away any excitement that makes sex great, and you will end up with a husband who plops into bed and says, "You wanna?" But if sex is a picture of intimacy with Christ, does this ring true? When we spend time with Christ, really getting to know Him, doesn't our relationship get sweeter and sweeter?

Shouldn't the same truth apply to our relationships with our husbands in regards to physical intimacy as well as every other aspect of marriage? If we spend time getting to know each other through having sex, communicating, showing each other new things, sharing our insecurities, and exploring what excites us, shouldn't sex get better and better? And isn't there always more to know? Sex on your twenty-fifth anniversary ought to be so much better than on your first anniversary.

Another example can be found in many marriage books. Well-meaning experts suggest a sort of bartering mentality with regard to sex.

Husbands are told, "Talk to your wife! Spend time with her! Serve her by helping with the dishes and taking out the trash. And if you do, you might just get lucky." I can only imagine how many husbands felt disillusioned when their wives didn't meet them wearing lingerie after the toilet was scrubbed.

Meanwhile, wives are told to have sex with their husbands so that they feel loved. "Have sex with him, and then he'll have deep, meaningful conversations with you, and help around the house!" If you buy into using sex as a way to get what you want, or withhold it when you don't get what you want, then you're bartering for sex; and pretty soon, you just feel used.

God doesn't barter with us. He doesn't say, "You do this for Me, and in return I will do that for you. Act a certain way, and then I will love you." Matthew 20:28 says that, "just as the Son of Man did not come to be served, but to serve, and to give his life as a ransom for many."

God loves us regardless of what we do—whether or not we remember to read our Bible, pray every day, or feed the hungry. Of course, if we spend time in God's Word, talk with Him regularly, and love and care for others, our relationship will only improve! In the same way, spending time with our spouses and meeting their needs makes our marriages healthier. Just as God's desire for intimacy with us is not based on our works, our willingness to engage in intimacy with our spouses cannot be based on their successful satisfaction of a list of demands. We cannot barter with our husbands because God does not barter with us. We are supposed to love each other regardless of what our spouses do for us.

## Turning Your Life Upside Down

Jesus repeatedly turned the world upside down and comparing intimacy with Christ to intimacy in marriage will turn your world upside down too. He said in Matthew 23:11, "The greatest among you will be your servant." Laying down your life is not easy. Creating the sex life that God wants for you will not come naturally, intuitively, or easily. You and your husband will have to trust each other, and you may have to be the first one to step forward by being courageous enough to trust your husband's intentions.

Serving your husband, regardless of his actions or reactions, will stretch you beyond what you can do on your own. Working on your sex life will drive you toward a new dependence on God. Intimately sharing yourself can only happen when you ground yourself in God's love.

## Finding God

While figuring out how to have a better sex life with my husband, I found God—or, should I say, He found me. I've been a Christian my entire life. Besides a short stint of rebellion during college, I have always been connected to a church body. Still, my relationship with God was more intellectual than relational. I knew God with my mind, but not so much with my heart.

Creating an intimate sex life with Jim taught me the difference between checking God off the "to do" list and pursuing a heart connection. My husband has never wanted me to have sex for the sake of fulfilling my duties. If I just went through the motions, sex felt empty to him. My husband cared more about where my heart was than he did about having a sexual release.

Jesus made it clear to the Pharisees in Mathew 23 that God cares more about our hearts than our actions. For years, I felt guilty when I did not have my quiet time, read my Bible, or pray. God doesn't want me to read my Bible just to check it off my list. God doesn't care if I have quiet time at 7 am every day. He cares that I desire Him.

As I have fallen more in love with Jesus, prayer has changed to this conversation that happens all day long. When I need answers, encouragement, or truth, I read His word. When I feel empty, I worship Him and He restores my soul. God does not want to be part of your "to do" list. He wants you to fall hopelessly in love with Him. Going after intimacy with my husband helped me discover a deep intimacy with Christ.

In the midst of insecurities and weariness, I've crawled up into God's lap. As tears rolled down my cheeks, I've felt the steadiness and comfort of a Father who knows and understands me better than I know myself.

While wrestling with next steps for ministry, I've felt Jesus's fingers gently run through my hair. As I wept at His feet, His tender touch met my searching eyes with gentle assurance. "Don't you trust me?"

I have fallen head over heels in love with Jesus. He has captured my heart, and the more I understand sex, the more I know who God is.

# Sexuality and Spirituality

It might sound strange to talk about a connection between our sexuality and our spirituality. In fact, it might even feel wrong or sacrilegious. *God and sex in the same sentence? How can that be?*

Most of us have created a huge divide between our sex life and our faith. The world's corruption of sex through pornography or idolizing sex outside of marriage has caused us to disconnect great sex from faith. We safely stay inside the confines of being a "good girl," or we reduce sex to procreation. If we do enjoy sex, we separate it from God. We pretend like God can't see so we can play. Most of us cannot imagine that God looks down on us while we thoroughly enjoy freedom in our marriage bed and smiles. I assure you, He does.

*Ask your friends if they have ever thought about a connection between spirituality and sexuality. Have they ever thought about God being part of sex? Why or why not?*

# Sex Helps Us Understand God

God created sex not just to strengthen marriages but because it embodies who He is. God is a God of relationship—Father, Son, and the Holy Spirit—all divine, yet unique. Man and woman were created the same—both human, yet uniquely male and female. We were created as sexual beings and designed to yearn for relationship with God and with others.

Relationship with God does not necessarily come easily. We cannot physically touch God, smell Him, or hear Him speak to us . . . *or can we?* Is it possible that as we learn to let go of ourselves and enter into holy communion during sex, we learn what it means to let go of ourselves and enter into holy communion with God? Maybe one of the reasons God gave us sex was to help us understand how to connect with Him.

When I first studied Song of Songs as an allegory of God's love for me, I remember thinking, *So when I have an orgasm, that point in time when I am thinking about nothing else—not how I look or what I sound like—but I'm just face to face with my husband, THAT is what God wants with ME.*

Surrendering to an orgasm mirrors what it means to surrender ourselves to God. I stop worrying and instead of trying to accomplish a task, I just meet with God. Time does not matter. I let go of control and expectations and open myself up to experience something new. Understanding what it takes to orgasm has helped me learn how to worship and simply commune with God.

God created sex to not only unite husband and wife but also to provide amazing pleasure through orgasm for both husband and wife. Orgasm helps us understand God's character. He is not a stingy God. He is extravagant, beyond our wildest imagination. In Song of Songs 5:1, God says, "Eat, friends, and drink; drink your fill of love." In other words, get drunk on each other, and don't hold back. In marriage, He offers wide open pastures to play. Within His boundaries of marriage, when we enjoy the pleasures He offers, we better understand His extravagant love. As we step into the freedom He desires for our marriage bed, we understand the freedom He wants to give us from or our own brokenness. When we understand His unconditional love, we begin to live out of a fullness and abundance of God's blessings rather than a desperate attempt to measure up.

One friend who took Awaken-Love shared that the class did more to change her relationship with God than it did to change her marriage. She and her husband already had a great sex life, but she had always struggled to connect with God on more than an intellectual basis. All of a sudden, she understood how to connect with God on an intimate level.

Sex teaches us about intimacy with God. Think about the most intimate connection you have ever had with your spouse. God wants to love you that intimately! Sex helps us learn about intimacy with God, but our relationship with God also helps us discern God's truth about sex.

**With your husband, share some parallels between your relationship with Christ and sex.**

## Final Thoughts

My sexual awakening was spurred on by my spiritual awakening. So many connections exist between our spirituality and our sexuality. Taking God off of my "to do" list and falling hopelessly in love with Him helped me understand the importance of taking sex off my "to do" list. As I learned to surrender during worship, I learned how to be present with my husband during sex. When I started reaching for God when I was broken and struggling I realized I needed to reach for my husband when I felt sad or inadequate. Finding a sweet spot where I craved connection with God helped me discover sex that is not driven by hormones but by desire for intimacy. Learning to pray with God throughout the day helped me understand that I need to have an all-day love affair with my husband. Learning to intimately connect with Christ has taught me how to intimately connect in marriage.

## Action Items

1. Spend time brainstorming and make a list of everything that creates intimacy in marriage. Then on a separate sheet of paper create a list of everything that creates intimacy with God. Notice any similarities?

2. Read Song of Songs out loud to yourself. Imagine that you are the Beloved and pay attention to what the Lover says to you.

# CHAPTER 8

# Unpacking Lies

WHEN I BEGAN STUDYING and understanding what God wanted for my sex life, I quickly realized that a huge chasm existed between what I believed and what God intended. Sex felt like a duty looming over my head. Even though I enjoyed sex when we had it, I constantly felt obligated. It was as if a giant time bomb ticked away, getting louder and louder and louder the longer we went without sex. And the longer I went without it, the more obligated I felt, and the less sex interested me. I knew sex was important to my husband, but some nights I literally had to psyche myself up to engage. Resentment built to the point that even when I knew I should, I wasn't sure I could.

I don't think I resented my husband; I think I resented sex. I have the most patient, kind, and loving husband in the world. He never badgered me for sex or tried to make me feel guilty. Regardless of whether we had sex, he helped around the house, put the kids to bed, and happily rubbed my feet when I slid them on his lap. On nights I gave him a chance, he would patiently warm me up to make sure I enjoyed making love. Still, in the back of my head, I remember thinking, *Darn it, I need to have sex with him again.*

I know that I am not the only one who has struggled to desire sex. Women share that even when their husbands plan a nice date, they have a hard time relaxing. They spend the entire night worrying, *I wonder if he will expect sex tonight?* It doesn't matter what nice thing our husbands do, when we feel an expectation of sex, their serving us does more to turn us off than to turn us on. Sex feels like the price we pay at the end of a long day.

If God created sex for wives as much as husbands, then why does it feel like the booby prize?

## Early Messages

When women are asked how they first learned about sex, their answers are amazingly similar:

- My mom left a book on my nightstand.
- From friends on the bus.
- I don't know.
- From the sex ed class in junior high.
- I discovered my brother's porn.
- My mom sat me down for an awkward conversation.
- I was sexually abused when I was seven.

If it weren't so tragic, it would almost seem comical. No wonder women struggle with sex! Very few of us have had any kind of positive messages. Sex can often be shrouded in silence, crude jokes, awkward conversations, or shame that leaves us confused and misinformed. The messages we often received from our parents consisted of either "don't do it" or "this is how you make a baby".

Can you imagine how sex would have felt different if our parents had shared all the reasons God created sex for marriage? What if they shared how sex bound them together and refreshed them? Or, that they were comforted by and got to know each other through sex? What if they shared that spending time skin to skin helped them understand the depth of intimacy God wants? Conversations about sex have to go beyond "the birds and the bees" or "don't do it." We need to create a safe place for kids to ask questions and also create anticipation and expectation for a wonderful sex life in marriage so our daughters won't struggle with the same lies we have.

*Talk to your friends about how they learned about sex and how those messages impacted them.*

## Our Bodies

Many women feel uncomfortable with their own bodies. In contrast to little boys whose penises became their best friend during potty training, many of us haven't seen ourselves. Our genitals feel foreign, hidden, and taboo. Parents are either silent when it comes to their daughters' bodies or they just say "don't touch" or "wash your hands". All of these messages can leave young girls feeling ashamed and dirty about their bodies. And how we feel about our bodies when we're young, influences whether we enjoy sex later on in life.

For example, many women who seek advice on how to orgasm would rather use a vibrator than spend time touching themselves. While men know their penises like the back of their hands, self-exploration fills many women with shame or disgust. God crafted our bodies exactly how He wanted them. Psalm 139:14 says, "Thank you for making me so wonderfully complex." Our bodies are God's creation! We need to embrace our bodies as much as our husbands have embraced theirs.

These early messages about sex and our bodies form the foundation of what we believe about sex. They make us feel like sex is bad or that our bodies are off limits. Until we recognize the lies we've believed about sex and our bodies, we won't embrace the truth about sex.

## Overall Messages

If you asked a group of men, "What was the overriding message you received about sex when you grew up?" most would sum it up by saying, **"Sex is going to be the BEST thing EVER."** For young boys then, sex is something to look forward to. They heard people say this, they believed it, and it often came true.

If you asked women this same question, however, they would probably respond that people told them, **"Don't do it before you're married, but later, do it for your husband"**. Quite a contrast, right?

We had these messages pounded into us, and they affect what we believe about our husbands and ourselves. These messages even shape how we respond during sex.

# Don't Do It

In an attempt to protect girls from losing their virginity or getting pregnant, the church, parents, and society warn us over and over again, "Don't do it!" Youth pastors illustrate the damage premarital sex inflicts with stories of flowers losing their petals: each time we give a part of ourselves away, another petal falls off until eventually only a bare stem remains. They tell young girls that only *they* can save their flowers because boys have no self-control. "Guard the gate! Set boundaries! Protect your petals," they say, "Because boys will take what they can and leave you ruined."

But then we get married, and in an instant after saying, "I do," we are expected to trust our husbands and enjoy sex! And yet we wonder: *My husband was one of those boys...Isn't he still trying to take something from me? Does he even want ME, or does he just want sex? He isn't washing the dishes because he cares about me. He doesn't really enjoy rubbing out the tension in my shoulders. He doesn't really think I am beautiful. He just wants sex.*

We never really progress from gatekeeping to embracing sex as something that is amazing for us, too. We still suspect our husbands; every time they do something nice, we question their motives. We leave our husbands at the same maturity level as that 15-year-old boy who tried to push the boundaries when we parked to make out in the back seat. We continue to protect and guard ourselves instead of embracing sex as an amazing gift from God.

God intended for us to wait until marriage to have sex, but if we constantly hear "Don't do it," we only get half of the story. Girls need to hear about the awesome sex life God wants them to enjoy in marriage. Respectful knowledge about their bodies should equip them with realistic expectations that learning to enjoy sex takes time. We also need to challenge boys to live with integrity and honor and to treat girls with respect. Pushing boundaries with a girl may someday impact what she believes about her husband.

Another effect of the message "Don't do it" happens when Christian girls cross lines, sometimes from their own choice, but many times when pressured or forced. With few messages that God forgives and heals sexual sin, many girls just give up and become promiscuous. Eventually carrying lots of baggage, they marry and believe the lie that they ruined their sex lives forever. God can heal anything, even sexual sin. Even if you slept with more boys than you can count, or used your body to somehow feel loved, God wants you to experience amazing healing and create an intimate sex life with your husband.

## Do It for Your Husband

One of the most common messages women in the church hear about sex is "do it for your husband."

Sarah grew up in a conservative Christian church that stressed the importance of sex to protect her husband from temptation. She was taught that if a husband wasn't taken care of by his wife, he would look elsewhere. She took those lessons to heart, and when she married, she committed to never turn him away. For the first ten years of marriage things were okay, but as life got busier with children, resentment begin to build. For the next ten years, Sarah's feelings of obligation toward her husband began to turn into even more resentment. Bitterness joined her resentment and grew until Sarah couldn't even stand her husband's *non*-sexual touch. After twenty years of marriage, they ended up in a counselor's office working through her years of feeling used.

Though sex is a powerful way for husbands to connect with their wife, the men I've taught don't want their wives just going through the motions to fulfill their needs. They want their wives to enjoy sex as much as they themselves do.

Sometimes I wonder if emphasizing the importance of sex for men has brainwashed women to believe that sex is not important for them. What if God really didn't intend for men and women to be at such opposite ends of the spectrum in prioritizing sex?

Marriage books, pastors, and even the media constantly remind us of the importance of sex for husbands. But they never tell us how important sex is for wives. They never say, "God created sex for wives," or, "Husbands, you need to get to know your wife's body. You need to initiate sex when she's not too tired and when she has enough energy to respond. Lead with a sureness and steadiness that lets her know you desire her. Make a safe place to set her creativity free." We just hear that sex is for our husbands.

These two overriding messages, "Don't do it" and "Do it for your husband", constantly linger in the back of our minds. They cause us to question our husbands' motivations and keep our guard up. These messages brainwash us to believe that sex isn't important to us. Sex, then, becomes an obligation and a duty. But God created sex to make the two of us into one--to comfort us and refresh us. Do you believe this in your head or in your heart?

# Brainwashed

Whether we realize it or not, the world bombards us with messages that form our ideas about sex. Even seemingly small things shape us. For example, the media portrays sex outside of marriage as always magical and hot. The man sweeps her off her feet. Fireworks erupt for both of them, with simultaneous orgasms during intercourse for all. No mess, no fuss, and each party always look beautiful and put together. Meanwhile in marriage, some slob of a guy begs for sex as his brazen wife berates his advances. The messages resonate loud and clear. Hot sex happens outside of marriage while only pathetic, boring sex happens within marriage, if you're lucky.

Media teaches us that great sex runs on emotions, passion, and unbridled desire that only thin young people enjoy. It doesn't matter how many people you use or sleep with in order to satisfy your physical need. Just get as much as you can without worrying about the consequences.

Other messages include intercourse always works for a woman, old people don't enjoy sex, and sex will naturally just fall into place. These subtle messages creep in without us ever realizing them.

Not only do these messages affect what we believe about sex, but they also shape what we believe about men. We believe that men will know exactly what to do to make us purr. Stereotypes focus on men who only think about sex, are ready at the drop of a hat, and whose drive is never impacted by life circumstances. We also hear messages about real men who have done horrific things.

One night, the evening news aired a story about a man raping a woman. As we headed to bed, I realized I felt angry at my husband. Men hurt women all the time—rape, domestic assault, murder, you name it. How can men hurt women like that? How could he?

But my husband didn't. And even though he is a man, he is not one of *those* men. We cannot project messages onto our husbands. Trust your husband based simply on his actions and on who you know him to be. Your husband is the same kind man who would do anything for you—even when he wants to have sex.

**With your friends, discuss messages that you heard about sex from the media, from church, or from your family.**

## Lies of Misinformation

Sometimes the lies we believe about sex are not spoken but are assumptions we make based on the information given, or lack thereof. Even the silence surrounding sex in the church and our families tells us something: "good Christians" don't enjoy sex; only "those people" enjoy it. As you unpack lies, don't just think about what you heard, but about what you didn't hear too.

Many Christian women who save themselves for their wedding night feel like they have been fed a bill of goods. They assumed that since they followed God's plan and stayed pure, their sex lives would magically fall into place. On their honeymoon, many virgins feel disillusioned and confused as intercourse either feels painful or like nothing at all. Brides feeling nervous because of strong purity messages can even suffer from a condition called vaginismus resulting in painful intercourse. We need to prepare virgin brides with reasonable expectations and good information about sex.

The media constantly reinforces the misconception that intercourse will lead to orgasm for women. For almost 70% of women, intercourse doesn't feel like much without added clitoral stimulation through the use of hands or a vibrator. Christian women especially feel that intercourse is the right way to have sex. They might understand the pleasure they can attain while stimulating the clitoris, but surely once they get married, intercourse will be all that they need. Women can feel disillusioned and bitter, then, when that doesn't turn out to be the case. "I waited for this?" they might ask themselves. And to them I would say, "No, you didn't! God has a better plan for you."

## Paradigm

We grow up in a paradigm that leaves women with no right place to be with sex.

**If we enjoy sex, we are sluts.**

**If we don't enjoy sex, we are prudes.**

Girls living in the hook-up culture survive in this paradigm by taking sex out of their control. Many of them get totally drunk when they have sex. Then no one can call them a slut or a prude. "The alcohol made them do it." Many married women rely on a glass of wine to loosen them up too. Is it possible that we cannot equate being a godly woman with freedom in our marriage bed? Do we need wine so we can express ourselves during sex without fear of judgement?

The "Good Girls Don't" mentality stifles our freedom in marriage. We grew up snickering and ridiculing the girls who crossed those lines. We considered ourselves better than them. We say to ourselves, "I would never do that!" Then we get married, and we don't know how to embrace our sexuality and freedom without becoming one of "those girls."

Those of us who do enjoy sex wonder what's wrong with us. When we want sex more than our husbands, which happens in about 25% of marriages, we question not only ourselves but our husbands.

God wants us to enjoy sex. He wants us to have the freedom to explore with our husbands and express our sexuality together in the safety of our marriage bed. He modeled this freedom in Song of Songs, alluding to all kinds of delights. They express desires, arouse each other with words, day dream about each other's bodies, and hold nothing back. We ought to have the best sex in marriage. When we embrace God's truth, we can simply be ourselves. Good Girls *Do*!

## Final Thoughts

In order for me to believe what God wanted for my sex life, I had to dismantle what caused me to feel the way I felt. There were reasons sex felt like a duty or that I didn't trust Jim when he initiated. There were reasons sex felt wrong and somehow separate from God. Wrong messages about sex determined my thoughts and actions. Until I discarded the lies, I could not embrace God's truth.

Our world is filled with wrong messages about sex, probably more today than ever before. We must constantly recognize lies that have impacted us, but we must also speak the truth to others. We can make a difference by opening up conversations about God's design for sex.

## Action Items

1. Spend some time brainstorming every lie that the world has told you about sex. What messages have you believed about men? What has shaped what you believe about yourself? Name them and write them down. Recognize how they have skewed your thinking about sex.

2. Spend time thinking about messages you received about your body, both good and bad. How did those messages impact how you view yourself? Pray and ask God to reveal any lies you have believed and renounce them out loud. Then ask God to tell you the truth, receive it by saying it out loud, and thank Him.

CHAPTER 9

# Finding Wholeness

A HUGE PART OF MY TRANSFORMATION came from healing the baggage I brought into my marriage bed. Until I let go
of the shame, resentment, and insecurities, I could not embrace real freedom. Viewing sex through my past experiences
distorted my lens and caused me to hide, question my husband, and protect myself. I could've lived for *years* in denial.
Unless we have the courage to dig up our mess, we stay stuck
in the muck.

I remember reading Kevin Leman's book *Sheet Music* out
loud to my husband one night when I came to this passage: "I
can't tell you how many times in my private practice I've
been the first one to find out—the first person the abused
woman ever shared her misery with. It amazes me that a guy

who has been married for ten or even fifteen years doesn't know how much hurt is in his wife's past."[1]

Leman was describing me. I had never been abused, but an incident from my past filled me with shame from the time I was a little girl. My secret held enormous power over my life because I had never dared to tell another living soul.

That night, as Jim held me in his arms, I opened up for the first time. With tears streaming down my face onto his chest, I slowly told my story.

## Shame

When I was about 7, I remember hanging from the swing set in the backyard playing with the boy across the street. As my dress hung over my head we laughed at the sight of my panties. Childish play turned into quick peeks of showing our bodies to each other.

About a week later, he showed up at my front door with a neighbor boy, wondering if I could play in the hills behind our house. I remember feeling uneasy but embarrassed to say no or explain why I didn't want to, so I agreed.

The hills were filled with huge sprawling oak trees that we climbed like monkeys all summer long. But on this day, we hiked up the ridge to the tunnels kids built under the Manzanita bushes. I vividly remember laying on my back with my panties down. Each boy took turns pulling down their jeans and laying on top of me, pretending like we were having sex.

There was no penetration, no kissing, no coercion. But I knew enough to know that what I did was wrong. What we

---

[1] Kevin Leman, *Sheet Music* (Illinois, Tyndale, 2003), 27.

had done filled me with shame and terrified me. *What if someone found out? What if one of the boys told their friends?* Everyone in school would know the truth about me. After that, my goal in life became shrinking back into the shadows to avoid attention.

For years whenever I heard the F-word used on the bus, I thought, "They know who I am." I was so naïve. I remember years later learning how babies are made and wondering if I was pregnant.

It sounds so silly to talk about now. Lots of us experienced child's play situations growing up. For many, it is no big deal. But my child's play experience profoundly impacted my life. This was the dirty secret no one knew. It filled me with shame and stuck me in the back corner of the room trying to hide from the time I was a child.

Telling my husband about my hidden secret and then praying over that situation was one of the most freeing experiences I've ever had. It was the beginning of allowing myself to really be known.

Being known, *fully* known, is one of the most terrifying things we can do. We might let our husbands know most of us. Maybe 80%, 90%, or even 95%—but all of us? Well, that is a different matter. Yet if we are not known, can we ever really experience freedom? Fear still controls us when we wonder, *what if he knew? Would he still love me?*

We spend most of our lives pretending to be something we aren't and striving to measure up. God loves you, regardless of your past. We all fall short. He doesn't want you to just share the presentable parts. He wants you to share *all* of you—even your sexual baggage.

When I started opening up with Jim about my sexual baggage, it created intimacy between the two of us. Sharing my baggage felt scary and vulnerable. I had a hard time looking him in the eye. I am sure many times he had no idea what to say. Still, he held me in his arms, and he allowed me to talk and to pray.

Sharing baggage is not about bringing up vivid details that might feel painful to your spouse. We can reveal things in general ways from our past, and more importantly, how they have molded our present. We can enter into the Holy of Holies to pray and ask for healing. We can hold each other accountable and call out the ways we have seen God move. We create intimacy in marriage by sharing even our sexual baggage.

Women in class have shared situations that filled them with shame for years. I can see the fear in their eyes when for the first time they bring light to the darkness. Years of comforting themselves through masturbation that left them feeling dirty. Pretending to be the perfect dating Christian couple while secretly crossing line after line. Hiding years of struggle with erotica or porn while crying out for deliverance. As women in class tearfully share their stories with the group during baggage night, nods of understanding and words of compassion greet them. Shame loosens its hold when we bring secrets to the light. In community, we can hold each other up, urge one another on, and step toward freedom. The chains of shame begin to fall off.

## Identifying

Identifying the baggage in your life takes courage, focus, and sometimes revelation from God.

It is amazing how much we remember from our sexual past. I remember the first time I held Samuel Perryman's hand during a movie in the 5th grade. I also remember the discomfort of sitting like a wallflower waiting for some boy to ask me to dance at a seventh-grade dance. I can easily recall details of the unwanted touches on a date in the back seat of a car. I also remember poor choices I made while dating my husband and during our engagement.

*Think about memories from your childhood or dating-life and share them with your husband. As you process, begin to think about how those experiences left their imprint on you.*

## Unraveling the Baggage

Sometimes God unravels baggage like a huge ball of twine. At first you don't see any issues at all. You don't even see the knot. But as you gently unroll the twine, you realize that certain parts don't pull off so easily. Something catches and you know there's something there. The more you unravel things, the clearer the knot becomes, until it becomes so clear that you can gently untangle it.

That was how it was with the baggage related to my husband. What seemed a simple case of resentment because we had not waited to have sex until marriage turned into something much deeper. It took time to unravel the different layers.

As a teenager, I had committed to wait until my wedding night to have sex. But when I met Jim my senior year in college, I fell head over heels in love—so much, in fact, that when I walked in from our first date, I proudly announced to my roommates, "I am going to marry him."

Up until that point, I really hadn't dated anyone seriously. Boys seemed like an unnecessary distraction as I pursued my engineering degree. I simply stuck my nose to the grind stone and focused on school.

When Jim and I began dating, I learned that he had had two serious past relationships and had slept with both of them. In my head, I decided that if Jim was going to fall in love with me, I needed to sleep with him. So, I brought up the conversation of sex, prepared by going on birth control, and helped plan for the big night.

As I wrestled with my baggage years later, I realized I resented my husband because I was not a virgin when we married. Even though I initiated sex, I blamed him. *Why hadn't he acted as the spiritual leader and insisted we wait?* Eventually God softened my heart to realize *I* needed to repent. I took ownership for my actions and asked for forgiveness.

It wasn't until a couple of years later that I uncovered the tightest knot buried underneath all that twine.

Because I had initiated sex instead of my husband, it left me with two choices: 1. Jim hadn't initiated sex because he was trying to do things differently this time and wanted to be a better man. 2. Jim didn't initiate sex because he wasn't really attracted to me. He didn't really desire me or want me. He just married me because I was the good practical choice for a wife.

You can imagine which option I chose.

Ding, ding, ding! Door number 2. *You don't really love me. You don't really desire me. You don't think I'm hot.*

So for our entire marriage, I struggled to believe that my husband really desired me. I believed I was the consolation prize and that he really wished he'd married one of those other girls. I just made a good practical choice for a wife and a mom.

The truth is, my husband is crazy about me. He always has been and he always will be. I just couldn't believe it because of the baggage we'd created. There were reasons I felt the way I felt, and once I uncovered them it helped me to believe the truth. Instead of viewing my marriage through my filter of insecurity, I could trust my husband.

Some people might question whether reasons always exist for the way that we feel. I'll be honest, I don't know, but I think a lot of times there are. Usually, if you dig deep enough, you will find something that prickles your core.

## Connecting the Dots

Sorting through baggage takes courage. You have to allow yourself to pause and take stock of painful memories. Over and over I've witnessed women connecting the dots of how they feel about sex with what affected them from their past. Sometimes it is words that create baggage, and other times it is silence. Sometimes it is actions or even just the way someone looked at us. Even seemingly insignificant things can have a profound impact on how we view ourselves and feel about sex.

One woman realized that the one act she could never enjoy with her husband, giving oral sex, was the one line she crossed before marriage with other men. That act filled her with shame from her past.

Another woman vividly remembered her mother crying to her dad, "She's been ruined. How could they do this to her?" after she received a dirty phone call as a very young child. She didn't understand the phone call, but she clearly understood her parent's words. Even as a child she felt like damaged property.

Several women remember that as young girls, they walked in on their parents having sex. They immediately sensed they did something wrong, but what followed was almost more powerful—total silence. The incident left them feeling confused and filled with shame, believing sex was wrong even in marriage.

One woman clearly remembered her mom bragging about the new furniture she received in return for a month of sex with her husband. Her daughter learned sex was a commodity for wives to use and trade to get what they wanted in life.

Even well-intentioned purity talks can influence how we feel about sex. Void of messages about God's redemption and grace surrounding sexuality, we begin to believe the lie that God cannot—or will not—heal sexual baggage.

That's one of the reasons to talk about sexual baggage and share our stories. We practice sharing our testimonies of sexual healing because so many women need to hear them. They need to hear about God's goodness and power, even in the scariest, most vulnerable area of our lives. We need to give people hope by sharing our stories of finding freedom in our marriage bed.

## Fantasies

Some women struggle with troubling fantasies that appear over and over and seem to control us. These fantasies leave us feeling confused or ashamed because the content so drastically opposes real life. Rather than defining us or foretelling our future, these fantasies provide a window into past painful experiences or messages. When we uncover the layers of their deeper meaning, these fantasies loosen their hold and don't seem quite so scary. Let me give a simple example to help you understand.

Many Christian women fantasize about being forced to have sex. This doesn't necessarily happen in a violent way but might involve a husband insisting on giving a wife pleasure, while she thinks, *No, you can't make me enjoy it!* Eventually their bodies can't resist and they experience pleasure. The need for the fantasy comes from a deep-seated belief that good girls don't enjoy sex. If they fantasize about being forced to enjoy sex, then their bodies can respond in pleasurable ways because their conscience is no longer responsible.

Rather than looking at the surface of an ingrained fantasy, search for the deeper meaning. As understanding replaces fear, the fantasy loosens its hold. Focus on being present with your husband by keeping your eyes open during sex or by talking to each other. If your mind wanders, gently pull it back. Eventually you may even decide to stop rewarding the fantasy with orgasm. Focus on connection with your husband and give your mind and body time to learn to respond in new ways. For a more in-depth look, *The Fantasy Fallacy* by Shannon Ethridge is a great Christian resource.

## Sexual Abuse

I will never forget the woman who walked up to me during the intermission of a sex conference I spoke at. With her husband quietly behind her and tears in her eyes she explained, "I'm sorry, but I have to leave. This is just too painful for me. I want to do this for my husband, but you see, my father abused me when I was just a child."

My heart broke and before I prayed for her, I looked her straight in the eye and gently told her, "God wants you to be whole, for you, not just for your husband. When you are ready, you need to do this for you."

We have this idea that we need to figure out sex for our husbands. When we struggle with responsiveness or claiming freedom, or even healing from abuse, we think, "I'll do this for my husband."

The first thing I tell women in an Awaken-Love class is, "This class is for you. Not your husband or your kids or anyone else. God wants to bless you with this amazing gift and He is standing there offering it. Will you take it?"

Many women have suffered some form of sexual abuse. It takes courage to face the truth and to even name the abuse. Please seek additional help like counseling if you have suffered sexual abuse. Dan Allender's book *Healing the Wounded Heart* is one of the best resources available.

I am a firm believer that healing takes place in community. I have seen women with years of individual counseling make huge strides in healing when they join a group study or support group. Sharing and encouragement will spur you on to steps of growth. Even when you think you've dealt with the abuse, changes in your life can bring the abuse to the front of your mind. Continue to go after more layers of healing. God wants you to be whole.

## Forgiveness

Forgiveness is a huge part of healing from sexual baggage. God calls us to forgive others in order to lead to restoration as we rebuild trust. He also calls us to forgive even if restoration is not an option. Forgiveness keeps us from becoming bitter and resentful, which eats away at our souls. It releases us from keeping another's accounts and holding grudges. God wants us to forgive so that we might live!

The hardest person to forgive is usually ourselves. Somehow, we feel like we don't deserve forgiveness so we punish ourselves. We can't enjoy something because we crossed that line before marriage. But isn't that somehow trying to be God? *We know best, so we punish ourselves instead of receiving the gifts God has for us.* Can we let go of our pride and trust God in His goodness?

So many women enjoyed sex before marriage and then felt mystified, ashamed, and confused when sex within marriage did nothing for them. We somehow decide we must not deserve great sex in marriage or that God must be punishing us.

It's true that sex within marriage will never be the same as hook-up sex or premarital sex. Sex outside of marriage runs on adrenaline and the rush of doing something taboo. It provides freedom to go wild and express ourselves without the fear of rejection. We may never have to see this guy again or meet his parents.

Sex within marriage will take intentionality and work if you want to keep your sex life fresh for 10, 30, or even 50 years. You will have to communicate, learn new things, and be vulnerable. You may even have to work through your baggage. If you spent years sleeping with countless men in order to feel loved, valued, or simply to satisfy a physical urge, you may have learned to disconnect during sex in order to protect yourself. Before you can intimately connect with your husband during sex then, you may have to grieve over the ways that you used your body and others in your past. God will hold you and weep with you and He will help you learn to intimately connect with your husband. God wants you to have an amazing sex life in marriage as you discover true intimacy. When you turn down the gift of freedom in sex, you somehow deny God who He is and what He can do.

## Stories

At the end of this chapter, I am going to ask you to take a look at your own sexual history. To inspire you, I'd like to share two stories with you from my "baggage night" in class.

### Shelly

Shelly came to class because her friend dragged her there. Both women struggled to enjoy sex in their marriage, but not because they didn't know what hot sex was. On baggage night, Shelly decided to go for it. Struggles with sex had already put so much strain on her young marriage that she wasn't sure they would make it. Surrounded by a group of women she had met only two weeks earlier, she poured out her story while tears streamed down her cheeks.

Shelly had been part of the hook-up culture in college and slept with more men than she could count. When she met her husband, they decided to do things right and remain pure until marriage. Her friend had been part of her accountability group while they were dating, and by the grace of God, she had made it to her wedding night without crossing any lines. But after all that hard work, sex with her husband was awful.

Through her tears, I knew Shelly was ready for change. She felt little hope but wanted things to be different.

I gently asked if we could pray for her. As we gathered around Shelly, I challenged the women, "As God brings things to your mind, ask for it specifically. Don't just ask for peace or comfort. Go big." We prayed that she would experience intimate connection during sex. That sex would feel completely different than it had before. That her eyes would be opened to experience her husband in a new way.

Shelly missed the last night of the class because of a conflict. But her friend was there, and I will never forget what she said. As we processed what we had learned from the class, she said, "More than anything, this class changed what I believe about God. I saw God do a miracle. My friend Shelly is completely changed. She has experienced so much breakthrough in her marriage, and because of that, I have a new understanding of who God is."

Shelly was ready for prayer and transformation because she had completely surrendered. She had nothing else left but to ask God for help. She was tired of trying to change things herself and was ready to ask for a miracle.

Sometimes, women just aren't ready to face their past. They might be able to name their baggage, but it is shrugged off as no big deal. Women will casually say they want things to change, but they have no emotion attached to it. If I press them by asking, "But what do you want?" they beat around the bush. If you don't have the courage to name what you want, how will you have the faith to grab onto what God offers you?

When you are willing to name it, God can do something amazing.

**Go for a walk with friends and bring up the topic of "What do you want in your marriage?"**

## Emily

Emily showed up ready for baggage week. She signed up for Awaken-Love because sex had been a major point of contention in her marriage. She had worked on getting emotionally and physically healthy all year, and working on her sex life was the next step on her journey. Already she had opened up to the group about the unhealth of her parent's marriage and the shame of finding comfort in masturbation as a young girl.

When it was her turn to share on baggage night, she pulled out a list. "I've been thinking about this all week, and I made a list because I didn't want to forget anything. Can I read this?"

As we listened to her tearfully read about shame, lines crossed, and regrets, I was struck by how committed she was to becoming whole. She was ready to go for it.

I told her, "It sounds like you know what you want. I think you are supposed to ask. I want you to ask God specifically for what you want and we will pray in agreement with you."

Emily slowly nodded her head as the group bowed their heads in prayer. Then she went for it. Emily asked from a place of brokenness but also of belief. Her voice sounded absolutely sure that God could transform her. She asked for healing from different situations and messages. She asked for freedom in her marriage bed.

God can heal us from sexual baggage, but it takes work. One of the things I've learned from class is the power of sharing in community. James 5:16 says, "Therefore confess your sins to each other and pray for each other so that you may be healed." There is power in speaking it out loud. Whether you are with a close girlfriend, a group of women, or your husband, transformation takes place in community. Time and time again I have witnessed transformation in class from digging up baggage, sharing it with others, and praying over it. The women visibly change. They walk differently, dress differently, and smile differently. They might as well have the word "freedom" plastered across their forehead.

You don't have to take a class to experience God's healing. Grab your husband or a friend and take a walk. Share your story with them, and think about what impact it had on your marriage bed. Think about what you need and want. Then go for it and ask God.

Walking out transformation is a journey. Often women experience instant change that leads to hope and breakthrough. It gives them the belief that things can be different. In that wave of hope, they take a step of courage they never would have taken before.

But a month later we can wonder if God really changed us. *Did I imagine that I am different? Was it all just pretend?*

God *did* change us. Maybe we have lost track of what our lives used to be and have forgotten just how broken we were. Or maybe old thought patterns take time to reroute. We have to flex our muscles and step out in faith to create new memories and a new normal. We have to live out our faith every day and daily surrender ourselves to God as we ask Him to help us take another step. Sometimes we simply hang onto God's truths and step out in obedience of who He created us to be.

## Final Thoughts

God wants us to be whole. He wants us to experience freedom in our marriage beds, but we have to deal with our sexual baggage. Experiences have affected how we feel about ourselves, our husbands, and sex. If your ideas about sex don't line up with God's design, then you need to ask yourself why. There are reasons why you limit what you allow yourself to enjoy in your marriage bed. Memories from your past cause you to disconnect during sex. The insecurity that constantly rears its ugly head has a root. Those hurts that wounded and caused you to "stay safe" can be healed. Shame holds no power in the light. God can transform you.

You have to spend time identifying experiences that influenced you. Ask God to bring to your mind anything that you need to remember. Spend time wrestling with God and ask him to help you connect the dots. Speak it out loud in a safe community with a friend or your husband. Figure out what you want. Ask God for it. Then, in faith, step into that new truth.

Working through my baggage created intimacy in my marriage. When I talked and prayed over those areas, Jim knew me in a new way. I had to humble myself and take a hard look at the choices and decisions I made. Repentance came through my brokenness and surrender to Jesus Christ. It required me to forgive others in the most vulnerable area of my life. Praying over my baggage and asking God for what I wanted took courage to be known. It required the faith to believe God could change even "that." Being known during sex and vulnerably taking steps of growth required a solid understanding of Whose I am: God's beloved.

## Action Items

1.  Sit down and write a complete sexual history, including the messages you have received about sex, interactions as a kid, dating situations, and even words that impacted how you felt about yourself. Ask God to reveal what you need to remember and to protect you from what you are not ready to remember. Share with your husband in general ways about your past but more importantly how your past has impacted your present.

2.  Grab your husband or a friend to talk through realizations and influences in your marriage bed from your past. Pray together and ask God for what you want.

# CHAPTER 10

# Living in a Broken World

WHEN I WAS IN FIRST GRADE, my best friend showed me her dad's giant stash of *Playboy* magazine neatly stacked on the garage shelf. She climbed up on a chair and gingerly pulled a couple of issues down to sneak into her bedroom for closer examination. We crawled onto her bed, giggling and laughing as we turned each page with Chuck Berry's song, "My Ding-A-Ling" playing in the background.

Forty years later, after discovering Christian sex blogs that introduced new ideas for my sex life, I went exploring for information about female ejaculation using my trusted friend Google. Several videos immediately popped up to answer my questions and offer multiple gateways into the world of porn. Each click enticed me to watch more and more, until I finally slammed my laptop shut in a tangle of feelings.

When my husband came home from work, I immediately told him what had happened. Even in those couple of hours, the power of internet porn scared me. For my own wellbeing, I assured my husband if I ever saw porn again, I would tell him. I knew that complete honesty with my husband would help safeguard me.

*If you have seen or read something that you regret, have a conversation with your husband about what it was and how it impacted you. Pray about it together.*

## Our World

Pornography, erotica, and our sexualized culture have affected all of us. Many of us have struggled to gain freedom from porn or erotica even after we marry. Even those not affected directly may struggle to embrace God's freedom in sexuality. A Christian husband who fought for purity can't allow himself to look at his own wife's body. A Christian wife wonders whether "those things" are okay because we know what happens in the world. We separate God from sex. How can something so torrid or disrespectful be part of God's Sacredness?

Sex is powerful and fueled by God-given desires and drives. We live in a world filled with temptations screaming for our attention, yet what the world offers will never satisfy us; it only makes us hungrier. What the world offers creates loneliness, self-centeredness, isolation, and division.

God created us for intimacy and relationship. However, in a world filled with casual sex, we have no idea how to create real intimacy in our own marriages.

# Do We Want to Know?

I had just finished teaching about pornography in class when I thought to pause and simply ask the other women, "Does anyone have something to add?"

Just when I felt ready to move on, Esther quietly filled the silence. "We went through this," she said. "My husband told me just a couple of weeks before we got married that he struggled with pornography. I didn't really think much about it because I figured all single guys looked at porn. I thought that once we were married it would just go away. But about three years into our marriage, my husband came to me and said he couldn't stand it anymore. Pretending like everything was okay while secretly viewing porn was killing him. He wanted to be honest with me."

Esther continued, "I was crushed and hurt. I couldn't believe he had been doing this behind my back. How could I trust him again?"

She went on to share, "I am now helping my husband battle porn. He has other accountability partners that are men, but I am also his accountability partner. He doesn't want any secrets between us. Without sharing graphic details, he shares enough so that I know he is serious about change. Even though his struggles are hard to hear, I am trying to be a safe place for my husband to be honest."

She further explained, "My husband saw my devastation when he disclosed his porn habit and he never wants to hurt me like that again. He wants to stay clean for me more than any other person. Since my husband first broke the silence years ago it has not been easy, but his struggle with porn has gradually decreased."

With tears in her eyes she said, "Even though I have no reason to suspect otherwise, I sometimes still wonder if my husband is being totally honest. The battle with porn is not just my husband's battle. I have my own insecurities that put up walls to prevent intimacy. We have chosen to create a safe place to be honest with each other and to battle together. Rather than pretending like things are okay, I would rather know."

For a moment the room was silent, until one woman voiced what many others were thinking., "I don't know if I want to know," she said.

What a profound statement. Do we want to know? Or are we so desperate to hang onto our perfect lives that we cannot hear our husbands' struggles or share our own brokenness? We could go on pretending for years, banging our heads against the wall, wondering why we feel so lonely. We can only create intimacy when we know each other—and that includes the mess.

I am going to talk specifically about wives dealing with a husband's porn problem because that is one of the most common scenarios we face, but really it could apply to any bondage in sexuality, whether porn, erotica, compulsive masturbation, or something else. Regardless of whether porn affects you or your husband, it will most likely affect someone that you know and love. We need to educate ourselves and cultivate compassion for those that struggle with sexual sin.

## Educate Yourself and Cultivate Compassion

We begin by understanding what porn is, why people view it, and why they have such a hard time stopping. Until you cultivate compassion for those trapped in porn's tendrils, your voice will only drive them further into shame and bondage.

Most people started viewing porn as kids or young adults when a friend introduced them to it, or they fell into it by accident. In the old days, boys passed around an old *Playboy* magazine. Today phones and computers offer live-streaming videos that can instantly mesmerize.

Porn grabs young boys' or girls' attention and holds them captive. It can act as an escape from stress, reality, or insecurities. They often figure that when they get married, they won't need it anymore; and for a while, that may have been true. But when kids come along, or stress fills their lives, or they just never feel like they measure up, porn is an easy place to turn.

Reaching for porn is a little like reaching for that piece of chocolate. When women are stressed, frustrated, or bored, chocolate calls out to us. For a moment, we feel better, but the problem doesn't really go away. Instead, shame steps in because we should have had more self-control, right?

Porn is like this too. It's a coping mechanism, which is the opposite of intimacy. It is what we do when we don't know how to connect or let someone know us. Viewing porn never satisfies, nor does eating chocolate. It always just leaves us feeling emptier than when we started.

Porn is not about whether your husband finds you sexy or beautiful or whether he loves you. Don't buy into the lie that if you just had more sex with him or did what women do in porn, he wouldn't struggle. You could have sex with him every day and he could still view porn. You are not responsible for your husband's porn use. He is responsible for his own actions, just like you are responsible for yours.

Many porn users want to come clean. They know it hurts their spouses, so they hide it while hoping to stop before anyone finds out. Countless times they have prayed for God to take away their urge. Every time they fail, the porn drives them deeper into shame and using more of it to cope with the shame. When they finally get the courage to talk with a spouse, they usually test the waters. When disclosure is met with disgust, or, "How could you do this to me?", communication comes to a screeching halt. As hard as this may sound, the more we offer grace to the user, the more likely we are to get the whole story.

Most women who find out their husbands view porn feel angry, disgusted, deceived, or numb. Your emotions aren't wrong, but we have to remember that our husbands are not the enemy. Satan is. Don't deny your emotions, but remember the difference between, "I hate that pornography has a hold on you", and, "I hate you for viewing pornography." Until porn has been brought to the light, healing cannot begin.

## Battling Porn Rather Than Our Husbands

We battle porn by creating what God intended: intimacy. We seek to truly know our husbands and to let them know us. If we are going to know our husbands, including his struggle with porn, then we have to create a safe place. Our husbands are not perfect and neither are we. We must gently affirm that we want to know all of them—even if it is hard, and even if it hurts. We must share our own brokenness, fears, and insecurities instead of pretending like we have it all together.

Nothing about creating a safe environment is easy. We must become healthy enough to realize that a husband's brokenness is not a reflection of whether he loves us or thinks we're beautiful. Our worth must come from God and no one else, not even from our husbands.

Brokenness affects the marriage, whether both spouses know about it or not. When we get married, we vow, "For better or for worse, in sickness and in health." If my husband is battling something, then I want to help him. I want to hold him up, encourage him, speak truth to him, and be there even when he slides backward.

Are you ready to commit to that kind of intimacy? Many women say it is the hardest thing they have ever done, yet it was the beginning of freedom. It is the end of pretending and hiding. They grieved together, clung to God, discovered what grace is really about, and battled side by side.

*Ask your husband about the first time he saw porn.*

## Bring Up Discussions About Porn

As strange as this sounds, talking about porn needs to become part of normal conversations with our husbands, our kids, and even our friends. We need to remove the power of shame and communicate compassion. People who struggle with porn are not the enemy. The enemy is Satan.

You could say something like,

- "I didn't know so many people struggle with porn, both men and women—even Christians. It must be hard, feeling like you can't talk to anybody about it."
- "You know, when I was a kid, my friend showed me her dad's Playboy magazines. It must be so much harder now

with internet porn available on every phone or computer."

- "I feel really bad for Bob and his wife. They are going through a lot, but at least now they know what they are battling."
- I want to be a safe place where you can tell me anything—even if you struggle with porn. I would rather know than not know."

## Don't Become the Police

If your husband struggles with pornography or lust, the only way he will stop, is if he wants to stop. You cannot shame him into it, you cannot force him, and you cannot police him enough to make him change.

Though we cannot make our husband stop viewing porn, there are things a wife can do to help a repentant husband gain freedom. We have the power to either inspire or deflate. Even when you feel hurt, betrayed, or angry, your husband must know that you value his honesty and that you hate the sin, not the sinner. Communicate that you are on his side and that your greatest desire is for him to experience freedom and true intimacy.

A truly repentant husband will do whatever it takes to rebuild trust with his wife. He will offer full disclosure without sharing graphic details that cause pain. A repentant husband will seek accountability partners, counselors, or other resources for healing. He will gladly install filters on the internet or computers and make practical choices to minimize temptation. He will not just give his wife lip service, but he will make changes to gain freedom and rebuild trust in the marriage. He may have setbacks, but he takes ground back bit by bit through openness, vulnerability, and honesty.

## Affirm Your Husband for Sharing

The idea that a husband protects his wife by not telling her the truth is a lie. A strong husband has the courage to share everything with his wife—even his brokenness—and he has the courage to help both of them go after their own healing and wholeness. The couples who make real progress battle pornography side by side.

We need to get in the habit of affirming our husbands whenever they share something from the heart, especially a struggle:

- "Thank you for being brave enough to share that with me. I know that must have been hard."
- "Thank you for being honest with me. This is hard for me, but I'm glad you trust me."
- "Thank you for sharing. It helps me to feel connected to you."

Even when what he shared feels like it just knocked the breath out of you, remember that it was probably one of the hardest things he ever has done, so affirm him for his courage.

## Learn His Triggers

Most men have certain things that trigger their desire for pornography. It might happen when they feel stressed from work or feel inadequate at home. They might struggle when life gets too busy and they don't take time to connect with God or with you or friends. Feeling like a failure can drive a man to struggle. As a wife, you can begin to recognize his triggers.

During those times, reach towards him in connection. Provide a safe place for him to open up and share about what is going on and how he feels. Take him for a walk and hold his hand. Encourage him to connect with a friend. Fill his needs with intimacy and grace rather than with porn and shame.

## Take Care of Yourself

One of the most important steps in helping your husband battle porn is to take care of yourself. Do not go through this alone. Tell your husband you need a couple of safe, godly women to process this with--women who can point you to God's truth and pray for you. Educate yourself about pornography and seek out resources on healing. Meet with a counselor or support group. Forgive your husband because it is the best thing you can do for yourself, but also communicate your needs so he can begin to rebuild trust. Be honest about how you feel so he can understand the importance of getting clean from porn.

Work on yourself and on your own insecurities too. Consider these questions:

- Why does his brokenness affect how you see yourself?
- Do you believe that God created you beautiful?
- Can you be the woman God wants you to be regardless of anyone else's actions?

Seek out opportunities to connect with God and deepen your relationship because your worth must come from Him.

## Accountability

At some point during the battle against porn, you may decide to be part of your husband's accountability. One friend realized she could usually tell when her husband struggled because he seemed distracted and avoided connection or eye contact. She decided that she would rather know than wonder, and you may too.

Accountability with you will look different than his accountability with other men. Graphic details of how he slipped will only create pain and division. However, you can help him wrestle with what triggered the slip and work on how he could react differently next time. For some couples, regular check-ins make the process easier because no one has to initiate a conversation. Other couples just check in when necessary.

In some ways, a wife makes the most sense for an accountability partner, because the ability to tell your wife it has been a good week is a great incentive to stay clean. I would rather know that my husband will be honest with me within 24 hours than wonder how he's doing. The two of you will need to figure out what works for your marriage but be open to the possibility of playing a role in his accountability.

## Create the Sex Life that God Wants for You

Part of battling porn is creating a great sex life together. It is not about competing with porn; it is about creating something drastically different—the intimacy God wants for you. Pray over your marriage bed. Ask God to bless your time together and help you encounter each other in a new way. Stay present during sex through eye-to-eye contact, using words to draw each other back, and feeling each other. Generously serve each other and enjoy your spouse's pleasure as much as your own. Praise God after your connection and thank Him for how He showed up. Embrace the freedom God wants for you and create a sex life based on intimacy and not on performance.

## Believe What God Can Do

Getting clean from porn or lust can be harder than getting clean from drugs. Your husband must hate his life of lust and porn more than the fears he will face in his battle for freedom. He might take two steps forward and one step back. If he is truly repentant and moving toward healing, then God calls us to offer grace and forgiveness over and over. You literally act as Christ's hands and feet to your husband.

Battling pornography requires a multi-pronged approach: accountability, setting controls, and going after the core issues. Habits that have taken years to form may take years to break. Recognize his small steps of honesty, openness, connection, or taking his mind captive. Encourage him in order to spur him on.

Your husband may be in for the battle of his life, and breaking free of pornography might take a miracle. Do you believe that God truly changes lives and that he can change your husband? Can you speak it to your husband? Do you believe that God can heal you so you can trust and cherish your husband? Do you believe that God can restore your sex life and make it brand new? Ask God for what you want, take small steps of faith, and watch God show up.

## Final Thoughts

As my friend shared her husband's recent confession about porn, I couldn't help but feel hopeful. Though she felt hurt and it would take time for her husband to re-earn trust, one day she might thank God for his disclosure. Now the two of them could create real intimacy. Rather than pretending to be perfect, they could be honest with each other.

The hard work of helping your husband battle pornography is an opportunity for change and growth for both of you. Porn is fueled by hiddenness, deceptions, and pretense—the opposite of intimacy. Battle pornography by creating what God originally desired—intimacy, to be fully known.

The best thing we can do for our marriages is to discover how much God loves us, regardless of what we have or haven't done. Romans 5:8 says, "But God demonstrates his own love for us in this. While we were still sinners, Christ died for us". When we realize how much we have been forgiven, then we can forgive others. Our worth comes not from our spouses or our accomplishments. God loved us while we were still sinners. Allow yourself to be fully known to the Father, and ask Him to help you be fully known to others. Feel the depth of His love and ask Him to help you love others like He loves you.

## Action Items

1. Spend some time journaling about what the goal is in your marriage? Is it being fully known, or pretending and trying to keep a safe distance?
2. Write a note to your husband and tell him what you value about him. Encourage him and call out the man God created him to be.

# CHAPTER 11

# Getting Naked

YEARS AGO, I WOULD HAVE SAID I didn't struggle with body image issues, but that was a lie. I didn't struggle because I never even considered that my husband might think I was beautiful. By eliminating risk, I avoided rejection and instead buried myself in accomplishments. Because I never felt comfortable in my own skin, I hated wearing dresses from the time I was a child. If my husband complimented me or brought attention to my looks, I shrugged it off or even felt resentful. Even walking through the lingerie department to buy undergarments filled me with anxiety. Beauty was something I simply avoided.

God changed me when I took the study on Song of Songs. We studied the book as an allegory of God's love for us. Each week we read the entire book. And each week, I cringed at passages like Song of Songs 1:15 when God says,

How beautiful you are, my darling!
Oh, how beautiful!
Your eyes are doves.

I never related to being beautiful. I grew up climbing trees, wearing my brother's hand-me-downs, and playing baseball. Some of my most painful memories were being mistaken as a boy.

But these passages in Song of Songs were not Man telling me I was beautiful; it was God. Why couldn't I believe that God created me beautiful?

I had spent my entire life trying to accomplish or do things. I worked hard in school, played in band, strived to please my parents, and built things. Being beautiful to God was not something I could ever do or accomplish. I just was.

Realizing this simple truth that God had created me—unique, exquisite, perfect, without blemish or flaw—transformed my life. No longer was my worth based on what I accomplished. I was simply loved because God loves me. God created me unique and absolutely beautiful.

**With your husband, share past experiences that shaped what you believed about yourself.**

## Insecurities

Insecurities about our bodies can have a huge impact on how much we enjoy sex. When we hide underneath the covers, we limit what we experience. Instead of reveling in a husband's touch, we worry about what he might see. We limit certain positions or acts and constantly recoil in fears of rejection. Body image issues hold us back from truly connecting during sex.

In Song of Songs 1:6, the woman struggles with her beauty when she says,

> Do not stare at me because I am dark,
>     because I am darkened by the sun.
> My mother's sons were angry with me
>     and made me take care of the vineyards;
>     my own vineyard I had to neglect.

She feels self-conscious because dark skin in those days was not stylish. Many of us can relate to feeling insecure about our beauty. We so want to hold our husbands' eyes, yet we struggle to believe we do.

Notice the first thing the husband says to his bride, though, in Song of Songs 1:9:

> I liken you, my darling,
>     to a mare among Pharaoh's chariot horses.

Strong stallions pulled Pharaoh's chariots, but when they wanted the stallions to go really fast, they would fasten a mare in front. The stallions would get so excited by the mare that they would literally be driven into a frenzy.

In Song of Songs, the Lover is saying to his Beloved, "You are so hot, you drive me into a frenzy."

Part of a husband's role is to affirm his wife's beauty. But many of us aren't very good at receiving compliments from our husbands. Our first response usually sounds like, "But look at my _____" or "What about _____?"

We take our husbands' truth and discard it for standards created by the world. We choose to believe what the world says instead of what our husbands say.

Most men are pretty simple. They don't make stuff up, and they don't play word games. If they say, "You are hot tonight," what they mean is, "You are hot tonight." They simply say what they mean. We need to receive their truth.

Within marriage, when a husband and wife keep themselves pure, God's design works so well. God created women with a deep desire to feel beautiful, and He created men with eyes that go crazy over their wives. When a husband keeps his eyes solely on his wife and speaks words of truth to her, he can help her embrace her beauty.

I am married to a quiet guy. When I decided to embrace my beauty, I had a hard conversation with my husband, "If you think I am beautiful, I need to hear you say it. I need you to help me believe it." He replied, "Don't I say it all the time?"

Now I don't know if he had been saying it and I just couldn't hear it, or if he had been thinking it and not speaking it out loud. Either way, if you need to hear your husband say you are beautiful, it might be time for a hard conversation. Ask him for what you need. It's not that we want our husbands to make stuff up or say what they think we want them to say. We simply want them to speak out loud what they think in their minds. We want to know even their thoughts.

If you have been rejecting your husband's compliments, you might need to repent for not believing him or for paying more attention to the world's standards than to his. Ask him to forgive you. Tell him you want to embrace your beauty and that you need to hear his words. Assure him that you want to believe him instead of the world.

Within marriage, feeling beautiful is not just about believing what our husbands think but about living it out. Feeling beautiful includes tapping into the power of our bodies to tantalize our husbands. In Song of Songs 2:9 the Beloved says,

> My beloved is like a gazelle or a young stag.
>   Look! There he stands behind our wall,
> gazing through the windows,
>   peering through the lattice.

He can't keep his eyes off her! He's even peeking at her through the lattice.

If we have not embraced our beauty and we catch our husbands peeking, our natural reaction usually is, "Stop it!" We react as if our husbands are "peeping Toms" who are trying to violate us. We tell them to stop, cower in self-defense, or scold them. All the while, our husbands wonder why they can't get over looking at us.

Men outside of marriage constantly violate women with their eyes. Maybe men have whistled or catcalled as you walked down the street. Or maybe they haven't, and you assumed it was because you are not beautiful. Men's visual nature can feel like a curse because they don't always handle it well.

If your husband struggles with lust, it may affect how your husband views you or whether his eyes make you feel objectified. Your husband needs to understand the importance of guarding his eyes for you. If trust has been broken, it must be rebuilt; but his eyes are not a curse or a bad thing.

God created your husband's eyes and they are definitely a good thing. God created his eyes to arouse, to excite him, and to draw him towards you. When a husband keeps his eyes pure, a wife who lets him enjoy her body becomes his standard of beauty.

A pure husband, feasting his eyes on his wife, ought to make her feel beautiful. When I dress up for a date now, it thrills me to see my husband's jaw drop. Noticing my husband peek at me as I dress warms my soul. Giving my husband a thrill while bending down to work creates anticipation and playfulness. God designed your husband's eyes to affirm your beauty.

***Share with your husband the importance of hearing that he thinks you are beautiful.***

## Comparisons

Countless women struggle with comparisons. We compare ourselves to photo-shopped images lining the grocery store checkout. We know they aren't real, yet we still hold onto these unrealistic standards. Just like a man needs to keep his eyes pure, we need to keep our eyes pure. Feeding ourselves with these images will only fuel our discontent.

More importantly, women often compare their bodies to the previous versions of their bodies—their wedding bodies, their pre-baby bodies, or their pre-fifty bodies. Having babies, experiencing 40 years of gravity, and settling into a desk job impacts our body. Time does not stand still, and neither do our bodies. We can either spend all of our time grieving, or we can live for today. Your body is God's creation. It is amazing. Our bodies ought to awe us like a snow-capped mountain or a beautiful sunset. Our bodies can comfort broken hearts, serve the hungry, and provide endless pleasure with our husbands. Our bodies are a gift from God and we need to care for them and keep them strong.

Sometimes I think that loving our bodies wouldn't be such a struggle if we just spent time getting comfortable with ourselves. If we looked at ourselves in a mirror on a regular basis, our bodies wouldn't feel so shocking. I purposefully take time to feel my body as I am bathing myself. I run my hands up and down my legs, around my waist, and over my breasts to feel my skin. I stand in front of the mirror nude as I prepare for bedtime and take notice of my curves. If you feel uncomfortable in your own body, maybe you just need to take some time getting to know yourself.

I choose to care about only two opinions about my beauty. The first is that God created me absolutely unique, comparable to no one. He created me in His image. I am stunning both inside and outside and I am His beloved. Because I love God and my family, I strive to stay strong and healthy by exercising and eating healthy food so that I can live a full life and serve God. The second opinion is that my husband loves every curve, crevice, and wrinkle of my body. I want to thrill my husband by freely sharing my body with him. I want to tantalize and tease him with the curves that catch his eye.

Ultimately, the *only* person who can determine whether I feel beautiful is *me*. No matter what my husband says, he cannot make me believe I am beautiful. No matter what friends say, they cannot convince me I am beautiful. I have the power to believe or not believe that I am absolutely stunning. You have that power, too.

**Talk with your friends about what defines beauty.**

## Embracing Beauty

Embracing my beauty has not all been easy and has taken perseverance. One time I decided to perform a strip tease for my husband. Picture me—a tall, gangly engineer, dancing around in a seductive manner. It was totally outside of my comfort zone, but if you want to grow, you have to stretch yourself.

Honestly, I don't remember much about the experience except that it felt awkward for both of us. Here I was, dancing around trying to be someone that I wasn't. Trying to compete with something my husband had spent his entire life avoiding. We got through it, laughed a little, and talked afterwards. Even though I felt uncomfortable, I didn't give up.

Afterwards I thought about the strip tease a lot. I wanted to make a statement to my husband that I was his and we could have some fun. I decided to try again and this time, not try to compete with what you might imagine at a strip club. I wanted to somehow represent the hidden sensuousness and desires that I don't show to anyone else besides my husband. I wanted the strip tease to represent me.

The thrift store provided the perfect place to purchase the black pencil skirt, white button-up blouse, and glasses that a reserved librarian might wear. With my hair pinned up tight, my black silk stockings and stiletto pumps hinted at the pleasures underneath. On the big night, my husband's smile said it all. I slowly teased and tantalized him as I gradually transformed from shy, reserved librarian to a confident, sexy wife.

I may never do another strip tease, but having the courage to shatter boundaries removed barriers and helped me discover who I am.

## Walking in Confidence

Learning to live in the truth that God created me absolutely beautiful—inside and out—has been a journey. It has required me to shift my focus from the world's definition of beauty to God's goodness and His unique design of me.

When I started to believe that I am beautiful, I began to walk differently and meet the eyes of others with confidence. I started wearing dresses that I would have never considered when I was hiding. Shopping for bras and lingerie no longer terrified me but made me feel sexy. For the first time, I started wearing a little make-up to bring out my green eyes and high cheekbones. When people noticed, I didn't cringe; I simply smiled and thanked them. As I took steps and lived out who God created me to be, I became more comfortable in my own skin and more radiant to those around me.

I also started believing my husband's words and reactions to my body. No longer content with "under the sheets" sex, the view of our bodies fuels my arousal. My husband and I constantly remark, "Isn't it amazing how perfectly our bodies fit together?"

## Final Thoughts

I will finish with one final story. When my husband turned 50 I wanted to give him a nude portrait of me. It was my way of saying, "I love you and I am all yours. Enjoy!" I posed for a close friend that I trusted and it was kind of this surreal moment of, "Ok, this is my body. It is God's creation and I love it."

She painted a beautiful watercolor that shows the curves and lines of my body from behind. When I gave it to my husband, he immediately smiled, because he knows me so very well. The portrait hangs over my husband's side of the bed and constantly reminds me that God is so good.

God wants you to experience freedom in your marriage bed, but you have to fall in love with yourself before you can share yourself with someone else.

## Action Items

1. Spend some time getting comfortable with your own body. When you shower, consciously feel yourself. Spend time in front of the mirror thanking God for each part of you.
2. Create anticipation by teasing your husband with your body. Undress while your husband has a subtle view of your body or go braless in a soft tee that hugs your curves in the privacy of your home.

# CHAPTER 12

# Stepping Into Freedom

BEFORE MY AWAKENING, I had no idea how much freedom God wanted me to experience in our marriage bed. Though we explored more than missionary position, I felt uneasy expressing myself. At times I reined myself in out of fear of going too far or losing control. Where were the guardrails? Could we enjoy what the world enjoys? What was okay and what was not? How much pleasure was too much pleasure?

There does seem to be this connection between overindulgence and sin. You can drink one glass of wine, but ten? Well, that's a different matter. So, we hold ourselves back and only allow ourselves to enjoy sex this much or to be that free. We safeguard ourselves by disassociating with anything that has a connection to what the world does.

Is it possible that we are holding ourselves back from exactly what we need in marriage? Maybe the freedom that goes on outside of marriage is what God wants us to enjoy within marriage. God wants to give us a glimpse of His original intention of being naked and unashamed. Have we let the world's corruption of sex keep us from receiving an amazing gift from Him? This gift is so powerful that it will literally transform our marriages.

## Steps of Change

Change did not come overnight for me. As I recognized lies that I believed, I started trusting my husband. When I understood God's design, I measured sex by whether we were getting to know each other. Dealing with my baggage released a newness in me. Stepping into freedom was both terrifying and exhilarating.

It was not about trying to compete with the world. I wanted to claim the freedom God intended for us. I cared far more about connecting with my husband than about creating a show.

When I wanted my husband to watch me during sex, it wasn't an attempt to create a pornographic scene for him. I simply wanted to maintain connection through eye contact. I wanted him to know who I was rather than just enjoy stimulation. This was *me* opening myself up to *him*.

When I performed a strip tease for my husband, I was not trying to compete with strip clubs. I wanted to put a stake in the ground that said, "I want to be free"—to share my naked body, to entice, and to move sensually. This was me, no one else—gangly arms, big feet, droopy breasts, and a C-section scar. Though terrified, I wanted to give my husband permission to feast his eyes on me.

Most of us don't immediately go from years of believing and behaving like sex is a duty to embracing all that God has to offer. You might even feel overwhelmed by the divide between who you are and who God wants you to be. It's okay, sister. I am right there with you. Change happens one small step at a time. Stepping out into the water, grounded in truth, and steadied by our heavenly Father, we tiptoe in. As we get more and more comfortable, we wade in a little deeper.

But we have to take a step.

God cannot do it for us. Our husbands cannot do it for us. We have to gather our courage and go for it.

In order to change what has been normal for us, we have to take small steps of action that declare that things are different. If you have never expressed yourself during sex, decide to open your mouth and release moans or sighs as your body responds. If you always have sex in the dark, surprise your husband with a couple of candles. If you've never asked for something, listen to your body and gently move your husband's hand where you want it. If you always have sex in bed, send the kids to Grandma's and plan where you want the action to take place. Just take one small step that says, "I am moving."

It may take time to find yourself. First steps can feel forced or unnatural. Don't give up. Give it a few tries, lighten up, and have some fun. Until you try things on for size, you have no idea what fits. I went through periods of trying different things until I found me.

## Engaging our Minds

Christian women commonly ask the question, "If I keep myself pure, how will I even know where to start?" We start with our minds. We let ourselves daydream about sex. We think about what touch would feel good and what scenario would be exciting. Turn on some sexy music, tap into the creative side of your mind, and imagine what you would like from your husband. God made us creative, and we have to allow ourselves to imagine great sex.

Most Christian women probably don't spend much time daydreaming about sex. In fact, we might even believe it is wrong to think about sex. How would it change our sex life if every time we washed dishes, we allowed our mind to daydream about what we could enjoy with our husbands that night? We have power in our minds.

You can also find ideas from good Christian resources. The internet has made it possible to research books before purchase. (I have included a great list of Christian sex blogs and books on the resource page.)

God has given us freedom to explore and express ourselves, but where are the boundaries?

*Spend some time talking with friends about if there is a gap between being godly and sensual and why.*

## Boundaries

God created sex for marriage, between one man and one woman, to make them into one. Though God addresses no detailed acts or positions and places virtually no limits on what a husband and wife can enjoy, the Bible does address some overarching principles that affect us, whether we are married or single.

1 Corinthians 6:12 says, "'I have the right to do anything,' you say—but not everything is beneficial. 'I have the right to do anything'—but I will not be mastered by anything."

Nothing is supposed to master us. In other words, nothing is more important than God and what He has called us to. God has called us to love our spouses selflessly. If some act in the marriage bed has become more important than the feelings of our spouses, then we are misaligned. The act has mastered us.

## Lust

The Bible also constantly warns us against lust, whether in singleness or in marriage. Matthew 5:28 says, "but I tell you that anyone who looks at a woman lustfully has already committed adultery with her in his heart."

We might think only men struggle with lust because of their eyes, but women struggle, too. We just lust in different ways. We lust when we begin to wonder why our husbands don't sweep us off our feet like the hero in the romance movie. We lust when we wish our husbands were more like the Bible study teacher at church who prays with his wife. We lust when we become impatient with a husband who can never make our hearts pound like the men we read about in romance novels.

Lust sneaks in when we get lazy and resort to escape rather than working on our own marriages. Lust sneaks in when we buy into the lie that sex will not take work. We expect that our husbands will know how to make us purr without any help from us. Instead of talking, we pout and escape. When I realized that reading romance novels only added to my dissatisfaction, I had to take a hard look at my own lust.

Beyond not being mastered by something or lusting, the Bible doesn't give a lot of specifics about what we get to enjoy in marriage. Within the confines of a loving marriage between one man and one woman, God gives us a huge playground in the marriage bed. Just because God does not prohibit something does not mean that something is good for us. We are all unique individuals with unique bodies. Sometimes we have baggage that has wounded us. God can heal anything, but it does not always happen on our timetable. Deciding what your marriage bed looks like takes discernment in community with your spouse and with God.

## Mutual Consent

Ultimately, God created sex as an act of loving each other. No one should ever feel manipulated, coerced, or guilted into partaking in a particular activity of sex. It is okay to say no to something, but we need to communicate.

If we are not comfortable with a particular position or act of sex, we need to wrestle with why. What makes me uncomfortable? How have my spouse's actions impacted how I feel? What messages or past experiences have impacted how I feel?

Sometimes God heals us in an instant. Sometimes healing comes over time. Sometimes God leaves a thorn in our side that we learn to live with.

One woman from class gave lots of hand jobs to boys while in high school. When she got married, she knew this was something she could not do. The thought of this particular activity reminded her of a time she was not living God's best in her life.

After she was encouraged to communicate with her husband, she wrote a note describing in general ways how her past baggage still affected her. Her husband felt relieved, because all along he had been wondering what he was doing wrong. Sharing her baggage helped her husband know her intimately.

Rest assured that nothing exists that God cannot heal, so ask. Believe that healing is possible. He wants you to experience freedom. More than that, He wants you to experience true intimacy. Talk about things. Wrestle with the walls you have constructed. Be honest with your husband, and ask God for what you want. Make sure that whatever you enjoy in marriage is something that you both are open to.

## Does It Create Intimacy?

The most important question to determine if something is beneficial for your marriage bed is this: *Will this create intimacy between us?* In other words, will we know each other better after doing something, or will this activity create division?

We are unique individuals and unique couples. What might create intimacy for one couple could create division or a stumbling block for another. We must discern what is both right and good for us.

I implore you not to put boundaries where they don't exist. Study the Bible for yourself. Read what it says about sex within the context of marriage. Read Song of Songs and taste the freedom the lovers experience. Talk about what you desire and what your husband desires. Wrestle with why you feel the way you do and ask God for insight. Together decide what will draw the two of you closer.

## Masturbation

One example of a gray area in the Bible is masturbation. Many of us grew up thinking masturbation was wrong. When you search the scriptures, the Bible does not address masturbation. The passage people most often quote is Genesis 38:9, "But Onan knew that the child would not be his; so whenever he slept with his brother's wife, he spilled his semen on the ground to keep from providing offspring for his brother." Onan wasn't masturbating; he was having sex and pulling out. God was angry at Onan because of his greed, pride, and disobedience.

The Bible doesn't address masturbation, but it *does* address lust and control. We are not supposed to lust after anyone or any image for our own gratification. Also, nothing should control us. If we have a bad day, we should reach for God or other relationships, not a coping mechanism like masturbation. Beyond that, the Bible remains silent on masturbation.

Two very distinct attitudes prevail about masturbation: One attitude says, "Nobody should ever masturbate. It is selfish and self-serving. It can only cause trouble." The other attitude says, "Everyone should masturbate. It is natural and uncontrollable." What if God wants us to live in the tension of discerning what is right for *us*? What if He wants us to involve Him in decisions about our sexuality and consider masturbation as a possible tool to create intimacy in marriage?

Because masturbation is a gray area in the bible, you need to ask yourselves two questions: 1) Is masturbation something you are both comfortable with? 2) Does masturbation create intimacy, or does it create division?

Assuming you are both open to masturbation, let's look at some situations where masturbation might create intimacy or division.

- Some women have a hard time figuring out orgasm with their husbands. The more they try, the more disappointment, pressure, and anxiety they feel. Giving a wife the freedom to explore her own body can provide the breakthrough she needs. Removing expectations, coupled with the ability to instantly adjust stimulation, can help her learn to orgasm. Once she has learned, she can show her husband and they can enjoy sex together. In this situation, could giving a wife permission for self-exploration create intimacy in marriage?

- What about the husband and wife who are separated for long periods of time? Rather than toughing it out, they decide to have some fun and try phone sex. Assured of privacy, they begin to arouse each other. Using just their words, they describe what they would do if they could touch each other. They express how they feel as excitement mounts. Can you imagine how phone sex would stretch your ability to express yourself with words? Would it be a new way to know each other?

- What about the wife who doesn't always finish during intercourse? Frustrated and afraid to hurt her husband's feelings, she secretly takes things into her own hands. Could masturbation in secret ever create intimacy?

- What if the wife who didn't finish talked to her husband? Instead of finishing on her own, they agreed to do things together. Sometimes four hands work better than two. Could that create intimacy?

Couples must prayerfully discern whether masturbation would create intimacy in their marriage or not. If someone has struggled with lust or masturbation, then pray about whether opening this up could become a stumbling block. Masturbation without conversation will never create intimacy. It always should be discussed first.

Until my awakening, my husband and I never considered talking to each other about masturbation. We went about our individual lives and didn't involve God in our sexuality. When we started involving God in our decisions about sex, we entered into a new freedom.

*Ask your husband what messages he received about masturbation, share your own messages, and talk about what the bible says. If you have kids, talk about how you want to handle the topic of masturbation with them.*

## Final Thoughts

Before Jim and I started working on our sex life, if I was bored I would sometimes transport the two of us in my mind to a deserted island. Imagining what I found exciting created the extra push I needed to finish.

As I started understanding God's design for our sex life and I stepped into freedom, the draw of fantasy decreased. Since God created sex as a way to know each other, I decided I wanted to stay present. Instead of imagining what excited me, I wanted to create it with Jim. With vulnerable communication, our sex life got better and better. We talked about new ideas and explored each other's bodies with renewed energy and freedom. Rather than just focusing on mechanics, we worked on connection during sex. We even shared our fantasies and had a fun time creating them together.

One cold winter day I cranked up the heat and told Jim to put on his swim suit. I slipped into my bikini and gathered supplies. While Jim laid on the large beach towel soaking up the heat, I slowly covered him in suntan lotion. The smells transported us to the beach where we imagined us together having amazing sex that day—without the nuisance of sand.

Jim's fantasies, on the other hand, always had to do with cars. I could never quite imagine actually enjoying sex in a car because of my fear of getting caught. But one night I got an idea. I set up our van in the garage with votive candles on the dashboard. A laptop played a romantic comedy while we made out on the bench seat covered with blankets. As we watched the movie, we might as well have been parked at a drive-in movie theater. That night we played out my husband's fantasy in a way that both of us could enjoy.

If we want to get to know each other during sex, then we have to be present. Rather than settling for escape to experience excitement, create it together. Start talking about sex, have fun, laugh, and enjoy an amazing time of discovering each other. Step into the freedom that God wants for your marriage bed.

## Action Items

1. Decide on one small step of freedom that you want to take this week in your marriage bed.
2. Think about ways that you can incorporate your God-given creativity in your marriage bed.

# CHAPTER 13

# The Power of Words

WHEN GOD WOKE ME UP to crave and desire intimacy with Jim, I began to feel more. But it also required that I share those feelings with Jim and not hide them. I wanted Jim to fully know me—from intimate conversations I had with God, to insecurities about my beauty, to what excites me in bed. It has not all been easy. Nor has sharing always felt equitable.

My husband is very different from me. While I seem to have the need to share my feelings, he has a hard time even identifying his. The other day I asked him how he felt and he said, "Better." I reminded him that "better" is not a feeling, and he quickly replied, "Better than yesterday." I have had to let go of my expectations and resist pressuring him to share his feelings.

When I scrutinize Jim's words or overreact, my husband becomes paralyzed. We had times in our marriage when Jim stopped talking. He felt like he always said the wrong thing, so it was better to say nothing at all. I am learning to create a safe place for Jim to talk when he is ready. No matter what Jim does, though, I choose to create intimacy through vulnerably sharing my words.

Creating an intimate sex life required that Jim and I learn to use our words. Instead of just *having* sex, we started *talking* about sex. Our words communicated needs and desires, from fun conversations filled with anticipation to really hard conversations out of necessity. We don't use words only to talk about sex. We also use words to make sex amazing. Short phrases pull us back toward connection and staying present with each other. Sharing creative ideas that we spin in our mind quickly creates arousal and excitement in anticipation of sex or even during sex. Learning to use our words has driven the transformation of our sex life.

## Words for Communication

Most people don't grow up talking about sex. In fact, most of us can hardly say the words. Our parents called our parts "down there." Boys joked, girls giggled, and the pastor skirted around the topic at pre-marriage counseling. We marry and feel embarrassed, broken, or ashamed when things don't magically fall into place. We have no idea how to talk to each other about sex.

Jim and I were no different. Over the course of 20 years of marriage, we had few conversations about sex. The ones we had were out of my desperation for change; they left us feeling more uncomfortable than connected.

When we were young and newly married, my lack of sexual response felt like the white elephant in the room. On my own, I sought resources that provided some answers. We then settled into a comfortable truce of not bringing up the topic. Along the way, frustrations came and went—mostly in silence.

After 20 years of not talking about sex, beginning the conversation felt almost impossible. Words like "orgasm," "penis," "vagina," or "clitoris" sounded like some foreign language. Cries of truth and disappointment were shrouded in embarrassment and just felt painful. We had to muster the courage to overpower the urge to stay comfortable in order to start talking.

## Hard Conversations

Our first intentional conversations about sex mostly revolved around issues that I struggled with and could no longer ignore, such as being left physically unsatisfied after intercourse, wanting more variety, or desiring a different approach than "You wanna?" Like most marriages, I usually had to initiate the conversations. By the time I had the courage to talk to Jim, my disappointment or frustration often was boiling. Many times, Jim had no clue what was going on and felt whacked in the back of the head. Fortunately, he didn't give up—and neither did I—and we kept talking.

One of our most fruitful conversations about sex happened in the middle of a coffee shop. In a neutral zone with our emotions in check, we could hear each other, ask questions, and really explore some solutions.

We learned that hard conversations about sex probably shouldn't take place in the bedroom. Wait for emotions to settle, and find a neutral location like the car, a walk, or a coffee shop. Talk side by side, speak gently and use lots of "I" statements. Hold hands during the conversation to communicate that you are a team.

- Start by sharing your hopes: "I love being married to you and I want us to have an amazing sex life . . ."

- Then take responsibility by saying something like, "I don't know if you realize this because I haven't talked to you about it, but I _____. " Make sure to own what is yours, and be honest.

- Conclude with collaboration: "Can we come up with some ideas of how we might do things different so that . . ."

Writing a letter can also be a great way to initiate hard conversations. Gently share your hopes, needs, and desires, and take ownership for your part. Give your husband time to process what he's read, and then ask for a time to talk it through in person.

Things usually don't change unless you have the courage to address them. Involve God in the conversation by praying before, during, or after you and your husband talk. As you work through hard issues together, vulnerably sharing your needs and desires, you will create intimacy.

## Neutral Conversations

Communication about sex drastically changed when Jim and I learned to have neutral conversations not driven by disappointment or frustration. Creating opportunities to talk about sex simply to discover more about each other will make the hard conversations easier.

One of our major breakthroughs in communication came when I started reading sections of the book *Sheet Music* out loud to Jim. Somehow all those horribly awkward words did not seem as uncomfortable when I read them. The book also put us on a neutral platform. I wasn't bringing sex up because it was an issue. We were simply discussing ideas and concepts in the book.

I would read a section out loud and say, "Is that how it is for you?" Or, "That's not quite how it is for me. It is more like _____." Eventually Jim started reading, which helped him get comfortable saying the words, too.

Reading *Sheet Music* brought up many different aspects of sex. Jim and I talked and prayed though my baggage. We discussed different messages we received from our families or churches as well as the impact of those messages. We also learned about the mechanics of sex and discussed ideas that piqued our interest. Using the book as a launch pad for discussion was a safe way to tiptoe into the waters of sharing our needs and desires.

A class or group study can act as a great impetus to strengthen communication about sex too. In the Awaken-Love class, for example, wives are asked to process with their husbands what they've learned. Couples begin to share vulnerably about their past and gain a new understanding and compassion for each other. Topics that in the past might have caused defensiveness are talked about in a quest to know and understand each other.

As you and your husband work through the survey, be mindful of how you react to your husband's answers. Creating a safe place for him to share will help him be honest. Even if you don't agree, you can still respect his honesty in sharing his desires. Seek to understand and try to find some middle ground to meet. Taking the survey can blow the doors open on communication. Many couples report that learning to talk about sex helps them communicate in other areas as well.

Neutral conversations require that you create a safe place to simply be you. Respectful conversations void of the charge of emotions and free of judgment will allow your spouse to be known. They are the bread-and-butter, meat-and-potato conversations about sex. Neutral conversations help to make the rest of the conversations about sex easier.

## Fun Conversations

Some conversations about sex ought to just be fun. You can remember good connections or dream about future connections. Talking about sex generates energy and shares how we view experiences from our different perspectives. Consider conversations on a long road trip where impulses cannot be immediately acted on, leisurely talks in bed as you fall asleep, or sneaky conversations in a public restaurant. The energy mounts, you share a part of yourself, ideas build on ideas, and some of it might just come true.

**Questions you can use**
- What is the best sex we've ever had? Why?
- If you could have sex anywhere, where would it be?
- If I would wear anything for you, what would it be?

- When I think about hot sex, I think about . . .
- If the house were empty, I would . . .

Talking about sex is not supposed to be all hard work. It is supposed to be fun, create anticipation, and generate ideas. We have to be intentional in creating time to talk.

After Jim and I moved our last daughter into the dorms at college, we spent the entire ride home talking about sex. We dreamed about the fun we could create in an empty house and made a sad day into a fun day.

Another time, I remember grabbing my husband as he left for work and explicitly whispering in his ear what I wanted him to do to me that night. He spent the entire day thinking about how he would make it happen. I looked forward to it. He knew exactly what I wanted, and I got what I wanted. I call that a win, win, win, win. My words created anticipation in a fun way for both of us.

Talking about sex helps to keep things from becoming stale. If you don't know where to start, simply share some of your favorite memories. "Remember that time when . . ."

Maybe one of the reasons we hate talking about sex is because our conversations always center around hard topics, like not finishing, or finishing too soon, being rejected, or not having our desires met. We also need to spend time just checking in or dreaming about the future. The more we have neutral and fun conversations about sex, the easier the hard ones become.

*Pick a couple of the questions from the list above. When you are both relaxed in bed, have a fun conversation about sex.*

## Words for Connection

God did not just give us words in order to communicate about sex. God gave us words to enhance sex.

Words help us connect. They pull us back to be present with each other. You may not realize it, but many times we escape into our own heads. We get caught up in worry, wondering if we'll have an orgasm or if we should do something different. Or we become bored, so we imagine some romantic scene that gets our motor running. We go through the motions, create the friction required, and end up rolling over in loneliness because we haven't really connected during sex.

Speaking short phrases during sex can act as a great way to maintain connection.

**Try these phrases to connect during sex:**
- *Can you feel me?*
- *I see you*
- *Don't leave me*
- *Hang onto me*
- *Come with me*
- *Let's dance*

Encourage your husband to use phrases such as "I've got you," "you are so beautiful," or "just let go" at the right moment.

Speaking to each other during sex may feel awkward or foreign at first. It might even feel shocking as you step into a new level of intimacy. But if God wants us to know each other through sex, then we need to be there.

# Learning to Use Words During Sex

If you or your husband find that words don't come easily during sex, you could try some games to take the pressure off and create a fun environment for both of you.

## Two-Minute Poker

"Two-Minute Poker" can help you practice asking for what you want. It also helps you learn about what the other spouse likes.

Play a quick moving game like "poker" or "rock, paper, scissors" with your spouse. Each round, the person who wins asks their spouse to do something for two minutes. Then you play another round. The game tends to start mild and ramp up as you get bolder and excitement builds.

Maybe you need to hear your husband's words, "Tell me what you love about my body from the tip of my toes to the top of my head."

Maybe you love feather touches, "Tickle the insides of my elbow or backs of my knees with feather touches." If he doesn't touch you light enough, then next round, ask again and tell him, "Even lighter." As you respond in enjoyment, your husband will learn exactly how to touch you.

The game also helps you get comfortable asking for what you want during sex. "For two minutes, tease my breasts. You can touch anywhere except the nipples. "

You might even want to learn what your husband likes. You could ask him, "Show me how you touch yourself."

Vulnerably sharing what you want during sex creates connection.

**Play by Play**

Another game called "Play by Play", can help quiet spouses become comfortable expressing themselves during sex.

Plan a sexual encounter where you are in charge. Blindfold your spouse in order to help him tune into what his body feels and what he is asking for. Tell your spouse that you will do whatever he wants as long as he asks. And you'll keep doing it, until he asks for something different. Basically, it will force him to use his words to guide you in loving him step by step. This game will help someone put words to what their body is asking for.

Sharing words during sex takes courage. It requires that you let the most important person in the world see into the most vulnerable area of your life. Using words during sex will take your connection to a whole new level.

## Words for Arousal

Words arouse all of us, but they especially arouse women. If you don't believe me, just look at how women devour romance novels and erotica. We can read a book and without ever being touched or seeing an image, our juices will start flowing. Even as a teenager, I remember reading a steamy romance novel and becoming aware of my body for the first time. Many women say that a good book gets them in the mood for sex when nothing else seems to work. Words arouse women, and that's not a bad thing. We just need to figure out how to take advantage of that in marriage.

Now that's not an easy thing. Just like sharing our body with our husbands can feel scary, it can be equally as terrifying for them to share their words with us! First attempts may feel clumsy and embarrassing for both of you. Words are a real area of growth. Encourage your husband, be patient, and set him up for success.

Let me give you an example of using words to arouse and focus your mind on connection. Imagine you are lying in bed cuddling with your husband and he says to you:

*You know that cabin that we go to by the lake? Next time I want to go with just the two of us when no one else is around. I want to lounge on the bed and see the sun glisten on your skin. And as I run my hand up and down your . . .* Well, you get to figure out the rest of that story. The point is that when your mind won't turn off, one way your husband can help you get in the game is to spin a story for you.

Song of Songs is filled with words that transport the two lovers, constantly calling, "Come away with me", or, "Take me with you; come let's run!" They call to each other and transport each other.

Words are a powerful way to escape together when you can't go on vacation to Mexico or Hawaii. They transport us to a time with less responsibility and younger bodies. Words release us from the everyday drudgery of laundry, dishes, and work. The possibilities are endless, with no budget, time constraints, or fear of being caught!

In Song of Songs chapter 4, the man woos her on their wedding night with passages dripping like:

Oh how you beautiful you are, my darling! Oh, how beautiful!... You have stolen my heart, my sister, my bride; you have stolen my heart with one glance of your eyes ... Your lips drop sweetness as the honeycomb, my bride; milk and honey are under your tongue... You are a garden locked up, my sister, my bride; you are a spring enclosed, a sealed fountain.

Finally, she can't stand it and in Song of Songs 4:16 calls out,

> Awake, north wind,
>     and come, south wind!
> Blow on my garden,
>     that its fragrance may spread everywhere.
> Let my beloved come into his garden
>     and taste its choice fruits.

Words arouse us. They are powerful, but they don't come easily for most men, especially words like Solomon's. The goal is not to imitate Solomon, or anyone else for that matter. The goal is for a husband to share a little piece of himself and speak out loud what he thinks in his mind. When he views your body and he thinks, "I am the luckiest guy in the world," he can speak it! When he admires your curves, he can speak it. When he spends his afternoon daydreaming about what he wants to do to you, he can speak it. He can say it out loud and then bring it to life.

If we want our husbands to get good at using words, then we have to show him what it looks like. We must create opportunities for our husbands to see how powerful words are. We can do things like lie in bed and leisurely dream out loud about how a hot encounter with him might play out. We can fill in vivid details about what leads up to the encounter, what we would wear, his next step, and what you ask him for. Play by play, we bring it to life, teasing him and teaching him what words can do.

Some of us might think sex is all easy for men, but it's not. In order to create a sex life that *both* of you find passionate and full of life, your husband will most likely need to use his words. And there is nothing easy about that.

**Help your husband understand how words create arousal similar to his sight by sharing the impact romance novels have on you.**

## Story Starters

If your husband needs help learning to spin stories, try using story starters. You can say something like, "What if the next time we went on a date, you surprised me by picking me up at the front door? When I walked down wearing black pumps and sheer stockings with a seam up the back, your jaw just drops. You gently walk me to the car . . . and then what?" You can toss the story back and forth to spin a tale as hot as you want—until you're ready to play it out.

Story Starters are a great way to collaborate and learn what excites each of you. As creative juices get flowing, one idea builds on another. They help both of you get comfortable using your words.

Another non-threatening way to get your husband to talk is to ask him to tell a story about one of the favorite times the two of you had sex. Make sure the mood is playful and pressure-free. As he talks, encourage more details by asking him to fill in details like where you were, what you were wearing, what he did, how you felt, what you did, and so on. Be patient and in your best sexy voice, just keep asking for the details that add spice.

## Sexy Words

Many Christians wonder if it's okay to use sexy language, also known as "dirty words." That is between you and your spouse and God. Ephesians 4:29 says, "Do not let any unwholesome talk come out of your mouths, but only what is helpful for building others up according to their needs, that it may benefit those who listen."

What feels unwholesome to one person might feel intimate to another. If you never ever use sexy words to tear down others, could they create excitement in the bedroom? Sharing those words only with each other could serve as a private language that gets your motors going. Could using sexy words in the bedroom actually communicate love and passion for a spouse who enjoys it?

You and your husband need to have a loving discussion about this. Pray over what is right for your marriage bed. Words that bring enjoyment to some people might feel incredibly painful for others. The only way to know is to communicate.

Some couples find it helpful to sit down together and brainstorm three lists: every word you can think of for any kind of sex, every word you can think of for your body parts, and every word you can think of for his body parts. Include clinical terms, slang terms, and terms you have created on your own. Then cross out every word that feels like a turnoff to either one of you. Circle every word that acts as a turn on.

Be sure to talk about timing as well. If you are going to use words to create arousal, then you need to use the right words at the right time. For some people clinical terms act as a real turnoff, while for others, certain slang terms can shut them down in a second; but if the words are used when they are very aroused or when they aren't aroused at all, they might feel quite differently.

## Erotica

Many women struggle with erotica and can feel like they carry a dirty little secret. Even if they love sex, they feel broken or twisted. Their sex life with their husband doesn't begin to compete with what they've discovered in books. They constantly battle and try to suppress their urges, wondering why God won't change their attraction to words.

These women aren't broken. Satan has simply twisted God's design. Women have amazing imaginations and a capacity for words to transport them. Rather than escaping to erotica, they need to learn to tap into the power of words to create an amazing sex life with their husbands.

Understanding God's design has set women free to enjoy the way they were created. One wife decided to start writing erotica about the two of them to only share with her husband. Other women have opened up communication with their husband. Together they are learning how to use words to turn each other on by speaking stories to each other. If husbands only realized the power of words, they might work harder to incorporate them into the marriage bed.

Don't miss out on the eroticism of words because you think that Christians should not say such things. Within the marriage bed, enjoy all that God has given you. Dare to know each other in a new way as you stretch yourselves to use the power of words to connect.

## Final Thoughts

Jim and I talk about sex all the time now. No words embarrass us. No topic is off limits. We have created a safe place to explore who we are, share ourselves, and wrestle with what scares us. I can honestly say that Jim and I are not afraid to address any struggle that comes up. But learning to use our words has gone far beyond just communicating our needs.

Words help us to stay present with each other during sex. My husband's smile when I gently say, "hey", reassures me that he's right there with me. His encouragement, "just let go", at exactly the right moment pushes me over the edge. When my husband asks for what he wants, his vulnerability turns me on. Words create an intimate point of connection during sex. Together we create a way to escape together and "Come Away" as we tap into words. Transform your marriage by learning to use words to communicate, create connection and ignite passion.

## Action Items

1.  Read a sex book out loud to your husband and open up conversation.
2.  Spend some time talking about what words to use in bed. Make three lists—his body parts, her body parts, and every kind of sex you can think of. Cross out all the turn-offs and talk through the turn-ons.
3.  Plan a time to either play "Two-Minute Poker" or "Play by Play" with your husband. Make sure it is fun and lighthearted with no expectations.

# CHAPTER 14

# The Not-So-Little Things

Catch for us the foxes,
   the little foxes
that ruin the vineyards,
   our vineyards that are in bloom.
(Song of Songs 2:15)

LITTLE THINGS CHANGED my sex life in big ways. They weren't new concepts or particularly exciting ones; rather, they were building blocks absolutely required to grow intimacy. Spending time together, talking, laughing, and touching on a regular basis helped us stay connected. Practicing self-care rather than running myself ragged left me with energy for Jim. Creating a transition zone to disengage from my day of multi-tasking helped me wind down so I could engage in sex. Probably the most basic concept was that building trust with Jim helped me to relax and let go of control. The safer I felt, the more I opened up as I let Jim know me. These simple concepts formed the foundation for creating an awesome sex life.

Sometimes the basic practices are the most difficult ones to hang onto. We get comfortable and lazy and let things slide. Our most important human relationship ends up taking a back burner to more pressing matters. Satan would love nothing more than for you to become complacent in the essentials for creating intimacy in your marriage.

It is not unlike our relationship with God. In Mathew 22:37, Jesus states that the greatest of God's commandments is: "Love the Lord your God with all your heart and with all your soul and with all your mind."

We so easily agree with that verse, yet we constantly allow things to become more important than our relationship with God. Distractions creep in that suck up time and attention—television, phones, ministry, kids, careers, and hobbies—and pretty soon we realize just how little time we spend with God. Even as we commit to read His Word or pray, our minds constantly race ahead to our day. Satan loves to distract us with good things to do to keep us from God. We must vigilantly protect our heart and our relationship with God because anything and everything will get in the way.

The same is true about intimacy in marriage. No matter how much we know and understand God's intention for sex, we still have to do the little things that keep our marriages healthy. Satan is on the prowl and waits for us to become complacent. He is on a mission to destroy our sex lives and our marriages. If we do not protect our time with our husbands, it will disappear. When we don't take care of ourselves, we create a crack for Satan to wiggle into our thoughts.

Satan would love to keep our minds spinning so we can't re-fresh with our husbands. He will do everything he can to convince us that our husbands are the enemy. We can't let Satan erode our foundation by neglecting the little things. We might make do for a while, but eventually the cracks will grow and life will crumble.

## Time

When Jim and I had young kids, creating time together meant loading our girls into a stroller or on their bikes and taking a walk. As we decompressed from our day we reconnected so we could work as a team. Over the years, time together has meant everything from working side by side on projects, tak-ing bike rides, and going on regular date nights.

The most basic need for a great marriage and a great sex life is simply having time together. For many couples, creating time requires hard choices. One woman had a revelation when she was unable do the homework with her husband from class because of conflicting work schedules. They made a hard choice and decided to put their marriage first by align-ing their work schedules and enrolling their kids in childcare. How would they ever create an intimate marriage if they nev-er saw each other?

Our kids need to know that our marriages come before their happiness. How we invest our time, money, and energy communicates our priorities.

Friends of ours have a crazy life filled with five kids and constant ministry. When they are not hosting people in their house, they are helping to rake a yard or visiting people in jail. Their busy schedules could easily derail their marriage. Instead, they purposefully designate one night a week as date night. Sometimes they go to dinner or a movie, or they sit and talk about goals for the upcoming week. Every week, date night happens and their marriage has thrived because of it.

In-home dates can work, too. One couple meets in the bedroom every Friday night as soon as they put the kids to bed. Free of distractions, they spend time together playing games, talking, lying skin to skin, or having sex.

Another couple practices "couch time" every day for 15 minutes as they share about their day. They don't talk about kids or schedules; they just connect. During couch time, the kids know to keep themselves occupied in other ways because their mom and dad need time together.

A friend once told me, "Guess what helped us the most from marriage counseling? Our homework assignment included going on a date every single week." We all know that we need to make dates a regular part of marriage. We heard it in pre-marriage counseling and read it in every marriage book. Do we need to wait until our marriage is in crisis and pay $100 per counseling session before we take the small things seriously? The little things we often take for granted have a huge impact.

## Non-Sexual Touch

Non-sexual touch is a primary way that couples connect, but wives often create unhealthy patterns in marriage. I used to avoid my husband's touch for fear of leading him on and disappointing him. Allowing my husband to touch me only when he had a chance to get lucky taught him to expect sex when we touched. Not only was I missing out on the touch that kept my fire burning, but Jim's expectation of sex when we did touch began to turn me off.

Most men receive very little touch besides ours. Maybe they feel so starved for sex because they really just need touch, which is one of every person's basic human needs.

Wives must take ownership for creating an expectation of sex after non-sexual touch. Ask your husband if you can start holding hands, hugging, giving back rubs, and kissing—without any sexual expectations. Take him at his word if he says he will just hold you. Don't take offense if you suddenly feel him poking you. He can't control his erection, but he will stand by his word.

One of the small things that helps couples spend time touching is going to bed at the same time. You can talk about your day or exchange backrubs. You can lie on top of your husband and "squeeze out the tension." You can read the Bible out loud to each other and then pray in each other's arms.

Our lives easily fill with good things to distract us from great things. Invest in your marriage simply by spending time touching. You will reap the rewards.

## Eye to Eye

When Jim and I were young, we used to wind down from a long day of wrangling kids by watching television. One show turned into another, and by the time we went to bed, the only thing on my mind was sleep. I think back and I wonder how our sex life might have benefited by leaving the screen off.

Today we have Facebook, YouTube, Netflix, video games and a million other distractions. Our phones come with us to work, to the dinner table, on dates, and to bed. Screens capture our eyes until time disappears into thin air. Yet God speaks about the power of the eyes:

> You have stolen my heart,
> my sister, my bride;
>     you have stolen my heart
> with one glance of your eyes...
> (Song of Songs 4:9)

Eye-to-eye connection opens our hearts and our souls to each other. Years ago, my husband figured out that when I went into pouting mode, he could gently take my face in his hands and implore, "Just look at me." He knew that when I looked into his eyes, I would see how much he loved me. As I let him see my eyes, I couldn't hide anymore. I slowly opened up to share what bothered me. Our eyes reveal the truth.

Unfortunately, technology can prevent us from seeing each other's eyes for days. How many couples do you notice out for dinner, each with their nose in a screen? We are missing out on a powerful point of connection.

Although most of us can't live without our phones, we *can* create boundaries. For instance, you could ask your husband for a screen-free zone from 8 pm to 8 am. This would give the two of you much more time to talk, play together, and yes, have sex.

It isn't rocket science: if you want to have a great sex life, you need to spend time together. God never intended sex to be this very separate thing that we do. It is like we go about our week hardly connecting, laughing, or even seeing each other's eyes, and suddenly we announce, "Oh, we better have sex." No, sex should roll out of connecting all day, every day. You have to intentionally make it happen, because everything will get in the way. Screens need boundaries so eyes can connect. You get to decide. Is your marriage worth it?

*With your husband, discuss ways that you can set up boundaries for technology in order to increase connection.*

## Self-Care

When my kids were little and one day ran into another, I needed something I could hold up and pronounce, "I did this today." Self-care for me meant building furniture in the woodshop during naptime. Letting the housework slide and spending a few minutes creating something helped me to be a better wife and mom. Taking time for hobbies, exercising, or visiting friends can rejuvenate you.

If you want to give yourself to your husband during sex, then you need to have something left to give. It's easy to feel worn out from a baby who has not yet learned to sleep or from working two jobs. How can you enjoy sex when you can't even stay awake? Different life stages create challenges, but they shouldn't go on forever.

Women tend to be martyrs and not ask for help until they are at the end of their rope. Your husband wants to be your hero, but you have to specifically ask for what you need. General requests leave him searching for random targets and feeling like a failure. Set your husband up for success, and encourage him without pointing out how he missed the mark. When we bring up shortcomings, it feels like complete failure to our husbands. Eventually they just give up. Help your husband succeed, and he will try to give you the world.

Investing in bras and underwear can be a way we care for ourselves. How many of us finished having babies and realized our underwear collection consisted of giant white panties and old nursing bras? Take the time to groom and leave your skin smooth and sexy. It will help you feel beautiful and more at ease during sex. Rather than always putting yourself last, take a few minutes each day to feed your soul.

One of the most important ways to care for yourself is by staying connected to God. Don't add another "to do" list to your schedule. Instead, realize that God provides true refreshment. Join a women's Bible study, play worship music, or just sit quietly for a few moments to listen to God. Grab the moments God gives you. See Him in all creation. Care for yourself by making your relationship with God a priority.

You cannot give yourself to your husband if you have nothing left to give. It's like the training we receive on airplanes: in an emergency, if the oxygen masks drop, you need to put your own mask on first, and *then* help others. Taking care of yourself is like putting on your own oxygen mask first. Don't fall into the trap of playing the martyr and putting everyone else ahead of you. If you want to honor God by how you care for your kids, husband, friends, or ministry, then take care of yourself first.

## An Oasis

For years, I struggled with sex during the winter simply because the sheets felt cold. The investment of a small inexpensive electric fireplace next to our bed heats our room and provides a little light and white noise. Small lights turn on with a remote, and our personal CD collection provides music. Within arm's reach, we stash coconut oil for lubrication and whatever else we enjoy. Our room is our sanctuary. On my bed, I meet with God and at night we meet with Him together. Our bedroom feels comfortable, soft, and warm. It helps me sink into connection with my husband. Pay attention to small details to create a great place to make love.

We need help transitioning from the chaos of the day to just being present with our husbands. After hectic days filled with wiping noses, doing laundry, working the cash register, dealing with work, or taking care of elderly parents, we have a hard time even thinking about sex. Late at night, our brain (still functioning on hyper-drive) already thinks about the challenges of tomorrow. Relaxing enough to engage in sex requires letting go of our "to do" list and trusting God with the details.

Try 20 minutes soaking in the bath in candlelight, a walk to burn off your worries, washing dishes while daydreaming about what's ahead, listening to worship music, dancing in your bedroom, or getting lost in a good book for a half an hour. Some women need to make a "to do" list to empty their brain, others talk things out with their husbands, and still others simply want silence. Figure out what helps you transition and ask your husband to help make it happen.

If you live in a chaotic world, creating an oasis in your bedroom can help you transition. Clear out all the junk that adds stress to your day—piles of laundry, unpaid bills, work projects, toys, and computers. Create a warm environment by investing in small touches like candles, artwork, or a new bedspread. When you step into your bedroom, it should make you relax and say, "Aaah."

Confidence in our privacy can help us in making the transition. Ensure privacy by installing a secure lock on the door.

Eliminate the need to listen for the pitter-patter of little feet or late-night teenagers coming home. Some women need a soundproof chamber located in the basement.

Our baggage affects even the level of privacy we need. One woman who walked in on her parents as a child still can't engage with her husband with their kids at home.

Do what you can to create the privacy you need, whether that means moving to a different bedroom, creating a sex den in the basement, or taking advantage of hotels. Also, try to see a lack of privacy as an opportunity for fun. Trying to stay quiet at the in-laws or taking advantage of kids being distracted by a movie can create newness and excitement. If you think life gets easier when kids age, realize that teenagers stay up all hours of the night. One of my husband's fondest memories was the surprise of me initiating when our daughter hosted a sleep over down the hall. Create an oasis in your bedroom regardless of what happens in the rest of the house.

***Brainstorm ways to make your bedroom feel like an oasis.***

## Trust

For our 25th anniversary, Jim and I traveled to Morocco to visit our daughter who was serving in the Peace Corps. We stayed in mud houses while visiting amazing countryside filled with stone-terraced wheat fields accessed only by donkeys. Needless to say, hot showers were non-existent. When we finally had a little privacy he said, "I don't even feel clean enough to touch you."

We build trust brick by brick, layer by layer. From the intentional choices husbands make for cleanliness to the lifelong journey of communicating our desires and longings, we start with the basics and build one brick at a time.

A husband who respects our need for simple hygiene and grooming creates trust. Our sensitive bodies require care. Rough fingernails or the stubble of a beard can feel like coarse sandpaper on delicate skin. A considerate husband will do all that he can to make us feel safe. A clean body, freshly shaven face, and smooth hands can make all the difference.

Few men understand just how vulnerable we feel during sex. Many wives have tolerated pain or discomfort during intercourse in order to avoid disappointing their husbands. An act so pleasurable for a husband can result in burning and pain because of inadequate lubrication, sensitive skin, or the slightest yeast infection. Worry or anxiety can cause our vaginas to contract during intercourse. Women are painfully aware that our husbands can hurt us during sex, whether intentionally or not.

In the midst of passion, even a loving husband can seem clueless about our discomfort. A clumsy touch or rough hands can feel like an intrusion as he pokes and probes. We tense up as his nervousness amplifies through our bodies. Guilt fills us for acting finicky or controlling. We hold our tongues to avoid discouraging them, or we hope they will just finish quickly.

We need to trust that our husbands are present during sex and that they are paying attention to us rather than blindly forging on with their plans. Watching facial expressions or sensing tension will help husbands identify the difference between pleasure and pain. When my husband started recognizing and asking if something felt uncomfortable, he built trust. I knew that he noticed and cared and was happy to adjust to make things enjoyable for both of us.

Trust needs to be a two-way street. Women have to create trust with their husbands by taking ownership and being honest.

Our husbands have no greater desire than for us to enjoy sex as much as they do. When we fake orgasm, we cheat both of us. When we refuse to invest the time to recognize lies about sex and learn the truth, we destroy trust. Taking ownership for figuring out our bodies and sharing that information with our husbands creates trust. Our husbands would do anything in the world to make sex enjoyable for us, but we have to help them know how.

As much as I want my husband connecting with me during sex, I don't want him to constantly worry about me. When a husband tiptoes around, constantly asking if something feels good, his nervous touch unsettles us and turns us off. What we really want is to feel his confident touch in tune to our bodies and fully taking us in. We want them to have the freedom to enjoy sex and get caught up in passion. A husband can't do that if he is constantly worrying. When my husband trusts that I will communicate, then he can let loose himself. My husband must trust that I will communicate honestly, no matter what.

Many women have experienced painful situations or breaches of trust in their past. We have tolerated unwanted touch and looks that left us feeling used and angry. Our own loving husbands might have pushed boundaries before marriage that left us wondering if we could trust them. They might have concealed a struggle with porn or guilted us into sex because of fear of relapsing into porn. Past experiences make us question whether our husbands care more about themselves than about us.

Most husbands fight an uphill battle to gain a wife's trust. They will need to prove with words and actions that they cherish their wives. They must respect our right to say "no" without even subtle manipulation. The more they take ownership for their own stuff, the more a wife will trust. When my husband asked that I forgive him for not helping us hold the line before marriage, we reached a new level of trust.

What God asks and what I desire—to submit to my husband—requires the ultimate trust. We can't really let our husbands lead until we absolutely trust them. We need to know that they care more about us than about a sexual release. We need to know that they won't become so consumed with their own passion and desires that they lose track of us. Our husbands must trust that we will honestly communicate our needs, even in the heat of the moment. We want to feel the sureness in a touch. We cannot pause in waiting or watching. We must have absolute trust in each other.

We have to create a safe place to enjoy sex—a basic concept that is the foundation for great sex. Deep down, we desire husbands who will lead, who will sweep us off our feet, and who understand what we need more than we know. We desire husbands who will take control, and with confidence say, "Let me do this", because they know exactly what we need.

## Final Thoughts

Prioritizing the little things that tend to get put on the back burner have helped Jim and me create the sex life we want. Even as empty nesters, our time seems to disappear. Eating meals together, holding hands while we worship, and going for walks are the staples that connect us every day. Taking care of myself by visiting with friends or buying sexy underwear helps me remember who I am. I look forward to spending time in my bedroom and disengaging from the day so that we can engage with each other. Breaking the doors open on communication has helped us develop trust with each other to take us to a new level of connection. Don't ignore the basic things that have a huge impact on your sex life.

## Action Items

1. Make a plan to better care for yourself so that you have energy for intimacy.
2. Focus on non-sexual touch and exchange back rubs.

# CHAPTER 15

# Discovering Potential

A WOMAN'S SEXUAL RESPONSE can seem anything but simple. At times it can feel downright elusive. I remember fighting back tears when my husband would collapse into pleasure while I still had no idea how to get there. Something that we assume will come as naturally as breathing air can leave us frustrated and feeling broken. Over time we eventually figure out our bodies, but even then, our response can feel like a game of Russian roulette. After a while, many of us begin to believe the lie that sex really is just for our husbands. We settle and accept our lot in life—orgasms once in a while when the stars align.

When I wrote the Awaken-Love curriculum, I was determined to provide not just spiritual answers that left women wondering why sex wasn't enjoyable for them. I wanted to provide thorough, respectful knowledge about women's bodies so they could create the sex life that God wants for them.

The truth is that our bodies were created to not only experience intense pleasure on a regular basis, but to expand our husbands' idea of what great sex looks like.

## Complicated and Good

God created women to be very different than men. What works for our husbands may not work for us, from the mechanics of intercourse to the pace of movement. Society has defined sex by what works for men, so we start chasing after the right physical technique or latest hot tip. The media's portrayal of mechanics and movement feels dizzying to a wife who craves connection. Remember our deep need for knowing? The answers lie not just in mechanics but in the power of connection—savoring each touch and connected movement while eye to eye, with spoken words. We need to figure out what great sex looks like to *us*, and then we need to share it with our husbands.

For women, many variables affect orgasm (physical, emotional and even spiritual). Some things are pretty obvious, such as the day of our cycle or whether we feel exhausted. Other things are subtle, such as sensing that our husbands are just going through a routine during sex or feeling like he's a million miles away. These things can wreak havoc and change our outcome. What worked great one day can do nothing the next day. We are complicated creatures, and we ought to have some compassion for our dear husbands who are trying to crack the "code."

The thing is that there is no "code." As much as we'd love to figure it out, it is like chasing the wind. What wives really long for is deep connection with a husband who knows her and will confidently lead her in the bedroom.

I don't think God made a mistake when He created women. He knew exactly what He was doing. In fact, Deuteronomy 24:5 says, "If a man has recently married, he must not be sent to war or have any other duty laid on him. For one year, (an entire year!) he is to be free to stay at home and bring happiness to the wife he has married."

God knew that He created wives to be complex. He knew it would take focused time and energy for a husband to learn to love his wife. That is part of God's design for sex. For most husbands, sexual response comes pretty easy. They basically operate with a simple on/off button, while we have a million knobs and dials to constantly tune and adjust. (see fig. 1).

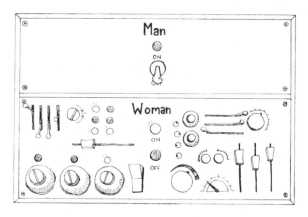

Figure 1, Illustration of the difference between Men and Women

At times I have envied my husband's simplicity. "God, why couldn't you have just given me a simple launch button? Why does sex have to be so complicated?" But truthfully, my husband and I would not have experienced the growth in connection, communication, and intimacy if sex were simple.

Part of the reason God created me to be complicated is so I can teach my husband the power of connection during sex. Instead of a straight-line path toward orgasm, we've learned to tease and tantalize each other to build excitement and discover new things. We express how we feel through sex by something as simple as how we hold each other. At times we courageously take charge and show the other what excites us. Connection creates as much arousal as mechanics and technique do.

Women's complexity creates a lifetime of new understanding, new experiences, and potential. Picture an old stereo component with many knobs and dials (see fig. 1). Our husbands get to play with every one of those dials and see what they do. As a husband learns how his wife's body, mind, and soul work, he can dial in sex based on who she is that day. Not just randomly set at the neutral positions, the knobs bring out the best in us for the song that will play. God created us with a million possibilities just waiting to be discovered. We have to embrace our potential, but it takes hard work.

It will require both you and your husband to grow. You will have to create new expectations and communicate about your desire. It will require you to push past disappointments and frustrations. You'll have to get back up and try again. Working on your sex life will be one of the most challenging and rewarding things that you do in your life, and it starts with you.

## Changing Our Mindset

We must discard the lie that God created sex for our husbands and that orgasm isn't important to us. I can't tell you how many books I've read that say, "Your wife doesn't need to orgasm. Sometimes she just wants to cuddle." You tell me, if you had a choice between "cuddling" or "orgasm and then cuddling," which one would you choose?

I am not saying that you have to orgasm *every* single time, but we need to be honest with ourselves and with our husbands. Do we really want to cuddle, or are we avoiding hard conversations and growth in our marriage? Do we really not care about orgasm, or are we just trying to let ourselves off the hook because we feel defective? Are we worth the time and trouble? Only you can decide.

You can redefine sex to work for both of you. Don't buy into the lie that sex will only be enjoyable to wives when the stars align. Your body is capable of amazing things, and your husband has not even scratched the surface. We have to believe that God created women as sexual beings to enjoy immense pleasure and connection.

Most husbands adamantly say they want nothing more than for their wives to enjoy sex as much as they do. Your husband can't make you believe it; only you can. God gave you a clitoris for no other purpose than pleasure, but you have to believe great sex is possible.

Great sex that lasts for years takes learning how your body works, being open to new discoveries, and communicating with your husband. Don't be guilted by the message that if you just surrender to your husband, everything will fall into place. Yes, we need to relax during sex, but we also need to have the right mindset, know our bodies, expand our definition of sex, and courageously share what excites us. Counter to what many of us have believed, great sex does not come naturally. It requires hard work for both wife and husband. We do not have to settle for mediocre sex that we enjoy only sometimes. We can create a sex life where both husband and wife thoroughly enjoy sex every single time.

## Defining Our Own Satisfaction

Scientists have studied women's sexual response for years in an attempt to define what happens. So many factors impact our response I don't how someone could ever simulate real, connecting sex in a laboratory. Rather than basing my understanding solely on what scientists have discovered, I choose to believe what women have shared.

Three thousand women anonymously answered questions about their sexual experiences in *The Hite Report* by Shere Hite. Women who masturbated reported they reached orgasm 95% of the time. Women also reported experiencing multiple orgasms during masturbation but rarely while enjoying sex with their partners. Make no mistake about it, women's bodies are capable of experiencing immense pleasure on a consistent basis.

One of my favorite books about sex, *Orgasms,* by Lou Paget, shares 10 pathways to orgasm: clitoral, cervical, G-spot, urethral, breast, mouth, anal, blended (more than one area), zone (a new arousal area typically developed by people with spinal cord injuries), and fantasy. This list doesn't serve as a "to-do" list of, "I got this one, but I better work on this one next." I share this list only to open up your mind to the breadth of possibilities. God gave you an amazing body, capable of experiencing pleasure through many different pathways. Don't limit what you experience. Maybe you will discover a path not even on the list!

Women's orgasm experiences vary widely. On a scale of 1 to 10, if men were to rate their orgasm it would probably be 8, 8, 8, 7.5, 8, 8.5, 8. Their orgasms all land close to the same point. If women rated their orgasms, I think they would vary all the way from 1 to 10.

Orgasms for women can feel very different. Sometimes we have a gradual climb of arousal ending in a sudden climactic release. Other times pleasure comes in waves that gently ride over us. Sometimes we can experience connecting pleasure that ebbs and flows and leaves us absolutely satiated. Don't discount your pleasure or enjoyment because you think orgasm should always feel the same.

Enjoy the connection and the different experiences with your husband. If you feel satisfied and content, you are good. If you want to keep going, then keep going. No one gets to define satisfaction or orgasm besides you.

## Knowing Your Body

God tucked our sexual parts away where we can hardly see them without using a mirror. We might feel like our bodies are random flaps of skin and crevices, but God gave us amazing bodies, including a clitoris that is capable of immense pleasure. If you really want to grow in accepting yourself, get out a mirror and see if you can identify the parts that make up your vulva (see fig. 2).

The skin around the clitoral head typically enjoys lots of stimulation. Gentle tugging or stroking of this skin creates the "bread and butter" strokes of arousal for clitoral orgasms. The ultra-sensitive head of the clitoris usually does not enjoy direct stimulation until highly aroused.

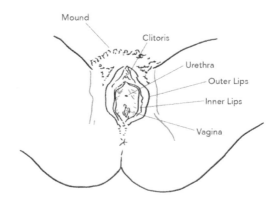

Figure 2, Vulva

If you pull the inner lips apart, you might see the urethra, a small hole inside the inner lips where urine exits the body. Lower down between your lips, you will see the entrance to the vagina. The outer third of the vagina, closest to the entrance, contains the most nerves. The inner two-thirds of the vagina, closest to the uterus, contain so few nerves that doctors sometimes operate without anesthesia.

In 1998, advancements in imaging helped scientists discover that the clitoris is made up of the clitoral head, a shaft extending towards the body, legs that come down towards the pelvic bones, and glans that wrap around both sides of the vagina (see fig. 3). When aroused, this system engorges with almost as much blood as the penis.

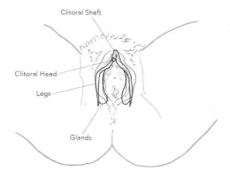

Figure 3, Structure of Clitoris

The clitoral head and the tissue around it are super sensitive. Small hangnails or rough skin can easily create pain, similar to a grit of sand in your eyeball. Contrary to what many of us believe, our bodies do not always create adequate lubrication, even when highly aroused. Always err on the side of too much lubrication to protect your delicate tissue. Coconut oil makes a great personal lubricant for sex, as well as protecting our bodies from both urinary tract infections and yeast infections because of its anti-fungal and anti-bacterial properties. With a little coconut oil on your fingers, gently touch the different areas of your body to learn how they feel. Realize that sensitivity ramps up as our minds engage and our bodies engorge with blood.

Women's vulvas vary dramatically in shape and color. Some women have inner lips that tuck inside their outer lips while others hang down as much as an inch. Color can vary from light pink, to dark purple, to tones of brown. Our sensitivities, though not dependent on size, also vary. While one woman might love direct massage of the clitoral head during high arousal, another might prefer indirect stimulation. God designed each one of us unique and special and just like He wanted us.

Our bodies are in a constant state of change, whether caused by hormone cycles or changes from childbirth or aging. Something you enjoyed one night might hurt the next simply because of hormonal changes. Our bodies go through enormous changes to birth a child. Scars and newly sensitive nerves require adjustments. Lower levels of estrogen due to nursing or aging decrease lubrication and make tissue less elastic. Changes can also awaken new delightful areas of sensitivities and discoveries. Be kind to yourself and compassionate to your husband as the two of you adjust to your constantly changing body.

## Learning New Things

A foundational concept to understand is that our bodies can learn new things. Whether we are trying to ride a bike, play the violin, eat new foods, or enjoy sex, with practice, patience, encouragement, and an expectation of good things to come, the possibilities are endless. The more we treat sex as a limitless, lifelong journey of discovery, the more potential we have to learn something new.

You have the power to create the sex life you want. A positive attitude coupled with focus, energy, and practice can achieve amazing results. The moment you get discouraged and doubt yourself, you take a step backwards. Include God in the process by asking Him to open you up to new possibilities and daily thank Him for every new sensation and discovery. Whether you are trying to have an orgasm for the very first time or are trying to experience more pleasure during intercourse, remember that your body can learn new things. Take one small step and move towards your desire.

Our culture teaches women that their husbands should take the lead during sex. Wives should lie back and relax while our husbands make orgasm happen. But think about what a man does during intercourse. When he wants to finish, he moves like he needs to move to get there. He engages his body and his pelvis, and he rubs his penis on us to create the stimulation he needs to orgasm.

In a similar way, we need to engage our pelvis, let our bodies move like they want, and lean into the pleasure. Rather than just receive, we share the experience.

I want to help you understand three different types of orgasm—clitoral, G-Spot, and Deep spot. These three types of orgasm will help us understand how to create more pleasure during intercourse, which is the topic for the next chapter.

## Clitoral Orgasms

Women who experience clitoral orgasm commonly say, "If you don't know if you've had one, then you haven't." Clitoral orgasms create the most physically intense, clearly defined orgasm. A pinpoint of pleasure builds and pulls you in until a sudden release of tension creates pleasure radiating outward. Women usually know exactly where the orgasm came from and when they are done having one. Clitoral orgasms are often accompanied by pulsing of the pelvic floor muscles, vagina, or sometimes even the uterus. Some women experience painful sensitivity of the clitoris after clitoral orgasm.

For most women, clitoral orgasms are the easiest to learn by using manual or oral stimulation. Gradually build tension and arousal by stroking and teasing the area. Generally, work from outer to inner, from less direct to more direct. Listen to your body and communicate with your husband.

Women who enjoy manual stimulation vary widely in the techniques used. Many prefer the flat pads of fingers smoothly gliding along the inner lips and around the clitoral head. Typical patterns include small circles around the head, side to side across, a couple of fingers gliding up and down each side of the shaft, or small tugs along one side of the clitoral head.

Rather than mindlessly rubbing over and over, women desire connection. They want a husband to feel them and know their body well enough to create excitement. Teasing can warm them up, circling back around can act as a reset when hitting a wall, and leaning into what really feels pleasurable can take them over the top. When a husband learns to read a wife's body, then a world of possibilities opens up.

Engagement of your mind gets the blood flowing, which creates arousal. Relax, breathe deeply, and get the blood pumping by alternately contracting and relaxing your PC muscles. Engage your body to create tension by thrusting your pelvis or tensing your legs. Allow your body to move like it wants to move. You might be surprised how much stimulation you desire. At the verge of orgasm, your clitoral head will pull back under the hood. At this point, don't panic, just stay steady to the end. Some women breathe rapidly, while others breathe deeply and some hold their breath in a moment of quietness as they search for the light at the end of the tunnel. Sometimes acting out how they experienced an orgasm in the past can trick their body into rolling over into pleasure. We are each unique and there is no wrong way to experience orgasm.

Self-exploration can help a woman who has hit a wall learn how to have an orgasm. Removing the pressure and expectation of a husband hoping for response can help a wife relax. Self-exploration also allows for instant feedback and adjustment as she learns what feels good. Once her body learns to comfortably respond, then she can show her husband and teach him what she enjoys.

For women who continue having trouble figuring out how to orgasm, the strong physical stimulation of a vibrator can help. The wife can then share that experience with her husband and make it part of their lovemaking. Learning how to orgasm with a vibrator may translate into learning to experience orgasm from manual or oral stimulation, or she might always use a vibrator to orgasm.

I will never forget reading the story of a wife who faithfully served her husband for over 15 years without enjoying the pleasure of an orgasm. On her birthday, she received a vibrator as a gag gift from a friend; she promptly stashed it away. One day, she pulled it out because she was curious. Low and behold, she discovered what she had been missing out on all those years.

Learning to orgasm takes time and practice. I have talked to many women who took months or even years to discover the pleasures of orgasm after they got married. To learn something new, you must practice on a regular basis, just like learning to play the violin. If you only half-heartedly tried once a week, then you would not make much progress.

Many women worry about taking too long to orgasm. On average, women require 20 minutes of clitoral stimulation to orgasm. That means for some women it might take 40 minutes. If you are learning to orgasm, I would suggest that every time you have sex or self-exploration, set the timer for 20 minutes. Until the timer goes off, your only goal is to see what new sensation or pleasure you can discover. Relax and enjoy touch in the most intimate way. Once the 20 minutes passes, you can decide if you want to keep going or not. Remember, your husband has no greater desire than for you to enjoy sex. Take the time and make the investment.

## G-Spot Orgasms

Women who have G-Spot orgasms describe a completely different experience then clitoral orgasm. They describe a full body orgasm, less defined pleasure, culminating in a bearing down or "pushing out" during orgasm. Science has discovered different nerve pathways for G-Spot versus clitoral orgasms, confirming that two very different experiences exist.

The G-Spot is located on the front wall (tummy side) of the vagina, about an inch or inch and a half in (see fig. 4).

Rather than a sensitive area on the skin or the surface of the vagina, the G-Spot is a collection of tissue deep inside. The G-Spot responds to firm stimulation by the pad of a finger in a come-hither motion, or from the head of a penis firmly pushing across it. G-Spot stimulation usually does not feel pleasurable until highly aroused.

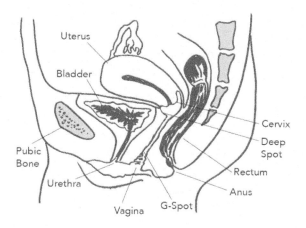

Figure 4, Cross Section of Female

Most women warm their bodies up with manual or oral stimulation of the clitoris before sliding a lubricated finger into the vagina. Slowly and firmly press into the front wall just behind the pubic bone with the pad of a finger and pull across the G-Spot. The area can feel like the textured roof of the mouth. As it becomes aroused, a smooth quarter sized area can bulge into the vagina. If you feel like you need to urinate during G-Spot stimulation simple empty your bladder beforehand and then try to relax. When G-Spot orgasm happens, your body will bear down and your vagina will push out hard enough to remove a finger. Stay firm and feel the waves of pleasure coming forth.

Scientists still debate about the G-Spot. They cannot dissect a body to find a unique structure or organ to hold up and say, "This is the G-Spot!" Women themselves are the ones who confirm the existence of a G-Spot orgasm. I choose to believe women.

Does every woman have a G-Spot? I don't know. Like I said, you can't dissect it, so you can't prove it. But imagine if you had an area deep inside of your body that had never been touched like it wanted to be touched. Maybe the first time you would think, "I don't know." But the next time you might think, "Maybe there's a little something." And each time, your body could awaken a little more to recognizing sensation.

Our vaginas also change and thin through childbirth or aging. Even if your G-Spot doesn't feel like much now, that doesn't mean it won't in the future, if you are open to new experiences.

*Discuss with your husband the differences between clitoral orgasms and G-Spot orgasms.*

## Deep Spot Orgasm

Lesser known than clitoral orgasm or G-Spot orgasm, women describe the Deep Spot (also known as the A-Spot) as a sure-fire rapid trigger for orgasm. Transmitted through the same nerve system as the G-Spot, Deep Spot orgasms feel very similar—a full-body pushing out of pleasure.

The Deep Spot is located deep inside the vagina, near the cervix (see fig. 4). Typically located on the front wall, some women enjoy stimulation on the back wall. Similar to the G-Spot, the Deep Spot responds to firm stimulation. The tricky part is it hurts if you bang into the cervix.

Some people use a finger to stimulate the Deep Spot. By following either the front or back wall of the vagina as far as you can reach, you can avoid hitting the cervix. Slowly, but firmly press into the area with the pad of a finger.

Others enjoy deep thrusting during intercourse at just the right time. Wait until high arousal when the uterus tips up and the vagina balloons out to create better access to the Deep Spot. Communicate or take control in order to find just the right angle to hit the Deep Spot.

As with the G-Spot, the Deep Spot is not an area that scientists can dissect. They cannot prove or disprove the existence of a Deep Spot. I choose to believe the experiences of women.

## Female Ejaculation

Years ago, women felt ashamed and embarrassed when they experienced a lack of urinary control during sex. Even though incontinence only happened during sex, these women were offered surgical procedures to fix the problem. It turns out these women may have been experiencing female ejaculation, a natural response for some women during intense extended sexual pleasure.

While knowledge should have created a sense of freedom for women, the world has once again skewed female sexual response. Pornography portrays women squirting across the room in intense moments of passion. Men now ask women why they don't ejaculate and create new expectations. There must be a happy medium. We need to educate ourselves about the capabilities of our bodies while resisting any new pressures.

Female ejaculation was mentioned by physicians as early as the 16th century but was largely ignored for years. Recent studies show conflicting conclusions, and scientists still aren't sure exactly what happens. Some think the peri-urethral gland that surrounds the urethra sweats a small amount of fluid into the urethra. Others believe the bladder produces a diluted solution similar to urine that is expelled. Once again, women's sexual response does not lend itself to hard and fast definitions. Regardless of what physiologically happens, let me share what I have learned from women.

Not every woman experiences female ejaculation. For those who do, it happens during extended high levels of arousal. They get to the place where they really let themselves go and don't worry about anything else. Sometimes female ejaculation happens during orgasm, but it can also happen before or after.

Female ejaculation is not an orgasm. It feels enjoyable and freeing but not necessarily earth shattering. It tends to be associated with G-Spot orgasm, probably because of the stimulation near the peri-urethral gland and the bearing down that happens during orgasm. Some women ejaculate a small amount and others expel enough to soak a towel. The ejaculate tastes like sweet water and neither smells nor stains the bed.

One woman I taught suddenly had a light bulb go on as I explained about female ejaculation. Early in her marriage, she had experienced embarrassment when she thought she had an accident during sex. Since that time, she no longer allowed herself to fully relax or enjoy things too much for fear of losing control. We can hold ourselves back by keeping our guard up and miss out on what God has for us.

We need to understand our bodies and what they are capable of and have the freedom to enjoy what God gives us. Empty your bladder before sex, and then relax and trust your body. Build trust with your husband, take down your walls, and enjoy whatever God gives you.

*Ask your husband what he knows about female ejaculation and share what you have learned.*

## Final Thoughts

One woman shared a story about an awkward situation during sex. This woman and her husband were enjoying sex and everything was going great. Eyes closed, lying on her back, she was enjoying all the sensations of missionary position. When she opened her eyes for a moment she suddenly saw her 3-year-old son riding her husband like a horse. In horror she whispered to him in a panic, "Honey! Honey!" And without missing a beat, he calmly whispered back, "It's okay, just ignore it."

And that is the difference between a man and a woman.

Men and women are different in so many ways, but especially in our sexuality. Just because you are different than your husband does not mean that God does not want you to enjoy sex. He created you with a complex body and response that can feel frustrating but also holds enormous potential for discovery and pleasure.

I am almost embarrassed to share how little I understood about my own body. I expected my husband to just take care of me. It wasn't until I started researching information about sexual response after a hysterectomy that I realized how little I knew. Knowledge has opened a new world and created possibilities that I did not even know existed. We need to know and understand how our bodies work, but we also need to resist limiting what we can experience.

Creating a sex life where both of you experience pleasure is possible, but it will take work. You have to believe that you are worth it and trust that your husband cares enough to invest in you. Knowledge is power, and you have the power to change your sex life.

Do the hard work of getting to know yourself, communicating your desires, and creating intimate connection, and you will discover a body that God has filled with potential.

## Action Items

1. Get out a mirror and dare to spend a little time looking at your own body. Identify the different parts and admire God's creativity.
2. Next time you have sex, try to discover a new pleasure point.

# CHAPTER 16

# The Big Question

"HOW DO I HAVE AN ORGASM during intercourse?" That is the question many women ask and the question I secretly struggled with for years.

I remember my young husband asking after intercourse, "Did you feel anything?" and thinking to myself, *Not really.* It's not that intercourse felt painful; it just literally felt like nothing. Eventually I believed this was just how intercourse was going to be, so we practiced the "she comes first" mantra.

When I began reading blogs about sex and the comments women wrote, I realized pleasure during intercourse was possible. Believing made the biggest difference in my ability to enjoy intercourse. Women hear that the mind is our biggest sex organ, and most of us agree. How many of us put that reality to use and transform our sexual experiences by engaging our minds?

Whether you have always enjoyed orgasm during intercourse or figure it will never happen, let me share some things to help make intercourse an amazing way to create pleasure and to intimately connect, regardless of orgasm.

But before we start, I want to share some statistics to help you understand the realities of sexual response for women.

## Statistics About Intercourse

About a third of women can orgasm during intercourse hands free or without any additional stimulation. About a third can orgasm during intercourse with some extra stimulation—his hands, her hands or a vibrator on her clitoris. About a third of women may never orgasm during intercourse.

Let me give you a whole different set of statistics. About a third of women can orgasm during intercourse almost all of the time, but they all do it all kinds of ways—hands-free, or with clitoral stimulation. About a third can orgasm during intercourse sometimes—when the stars align. About a third of women may never orgasm during intercourse.

The topic of orgasm during intercourse feels very personal to me. I remember when God first called me to teach Awaken-Love. I cried out to Him, "How can you ask me to teach a sex class when I haven't even had sex the right way yet?" At that time, I still had not experienced an orgasm during intercourse.

As Christian women, we can feel like there's something wrong with us if we can't orgasm during intercourse. The church doesn't necessarily even teach us that there's something wrong. We do it to ourselves. We create this hierarchy of sex: simultaneous orgasm during intercourse at the top, then orgasm during intercourse hands-free, orgasm during intercourse with his hands, and down the line until we get to orgasm during manual stimulation. God did not create a hierarchy of orgasm. Ranking sexual experiences is not biblical.

When we don't orgasm during intercourse, we can look down on ourselves. We think, *I might enjoy sex, but if I was really surrendered to my husband, if I trusted him more, or if I stopped being so controlling, then I would orgasm during intercourse.*

Many things affect orgasm during intercourse, and some are totally out of our control. Recent studies suggest the greater distance between your clitoris and your vaginal opening, the less likely you will have an orgasm during intercourse. That distance tends to correlate with height. Does that mean if you're tall and you've never experienced orgasm during intercourse, you never will? Not necessarily.

Some woman can orgasm through using their mind alone. We have to start with a fresh slate and believe enjoyment and orgasm are possible. Knowledge is powerful, and the internet is an amazing resource. Reading testimonies of other women gave me the courage to hope and to believe that pleasurable intercourse was possible. When we believe something is possible, we actually have a chance. Whether or not you ever have an orgasm during intercourse, I pray that you will discover an amazing way to intimately connect and enjoy pleasure together through becoming one.

*Many husbands do not realize the reality of women's response during intercourse and carry the burden of whether his wife enjoys sex or not. Share with him these statistics and your personal experiences.*

## Start Fresh

One of the first steps I took was to discard all my preconceived ideas of what intercourse looks like. Whether we realize it or not, we tend to model intercourse after how media portrays it. For centuries, sex has largely been defined by men and by what works for them. The skin to skin friction of thrusting the penis in and out of the vagina provides great stimulation for men, but it does little for most women. Wipe out any ideas that you have in your head of what intercourse should look like. Start with a clean slate and go on a journey of discovering what feels good to you.

Before I share some ways to make intercourse more enjoyable, let's establish some guidelines to empower you without adding more performance pressure.

## Guidelines for Working on Your Sex Life

1. There is no "right way" to have sex or to orgasm. God created it all and it is all good.
2. There is no magic formula. We are all very different.
3. Enjoy the journey. If you have become so goal-focused or frustrated that you do not connect with your spouse, you need to take a step back from trying and focus on connection.
4. Get rid of all preconceived notions of what intercourse looks like. What you see in the movies works for men, but not for women. Allow yourself to explore outside of the box and discover what you enjoy.
5. Let go of the control, and don't try so hard. Be present and ask God to help you just relax and enjoy the ride

6. Never say never. If you have never experienced an orgasm during intercourse, you need to believe that it can still happen. In fact, you need to start imagining it happening. The minute you say it will never happen is the minute you shut yourself down.

Regardless of whether we orgasm during intercourse or not, intercourse should be enjoyable and connecting for both of you. (If intercourse is painful, seek the help of a doctor or pelvic floor therapist. Don't give up until you get some answers.) Intercourse is God's design to make what seems like an impossibility an opportunity for growth. Ask your husband to let you take charge for a while, and along the way, you might just show him something new.

I want to share some specific things that can help you enjoy intercourse more.

## Get Your Body in Shape

The older I get, the more I understand the importance to keeping my body in shape. Stronger Kegels mean stronger orgasms and an increased chance of orgasm during intercourse. A strong body, abs, legs, butt, or back will help you move for as long as you want. Don't just lie there during intercourse. Get involved. Move in circles, from side to side, or whatever feels good.

## Slow Down

Intercourse often seems like a blur of motion that feels like nothing. The best advice a friend shared was to just slow down. Start by getting him inside of you and be still. Allow your body to wake up and let him acclimate to a wonderful warm place and just settle in. Establish connection with each other. Think about *feeling* your husband instead of just rubbing him. In order to do that, you have to move slowly. Really slowly. You have to meld your body to his body, not just penis to vagina, but every part that wants to meet. Once you start moving, pay attention to your body and figure out what feels good. Slowly and intentionally, find ways to rub your clitoris on him, or stimulate your vagina using his penis.

## Simplify

Sometimes more is not necessarily better. Yes, you can stimulate the clitoris, the breasts, the vagina, and the lips at the same time. You can also add stimulation using hands or a vibrator. Every once in a while, take a step back and just focus on one area or one sensation at a time. Breathe deeply, relax, and take it in. Be patient and allow your body to wake up. Then slowly lean in to what feels good. See what you can discover and how far you can ride it.

## Visualize

Spend time dreaming and visualizing what would feel good during intercourse. What spots would he hit with his penis? How fast would he move? How would you move? What would his body feel like? How would he hold you? How would things ramp up as you accelerated toward climax? What would it feel like when you came? Imagine pleasure and even orgasm happening.

## Create Positive Connections

Move toward believing that intercourse can be pleasurable by using your husband's penis to create pleasure other ways. Straddle your husband, lube yourself up and use his penis to stimulate your clitoris. Push the head all over and enjoy the sensations. Create a tunnel between your hand and your vulva for his penis to slowly pass through. Have your husband lie on top of you with the head of his penis pressed into your clitoris. As you feel him press into you, slowly push your pelvis against him, breathe deeply, feel his body cover yours, and see how aroused you can get. Associate pleasure with his penis.

## Explore Pleasure Spots

Spend some time exploring with your husband what feels good during intercourse. Have your husband enter you and then both of you lie still. Can you feel his penis inside of you? Can he feel your vagina? Squeeze your husband's shaft with your Kegel muscles. What does it feel like? Have your husband position himself so that the head of his penis is barely in your vagina. How does it feel? How about a little deeper? How about angled toward your front wall? What does it feel like when his body is pressed completely against yours? Can you feel pressure on your clitoris? Experiment with different movements and tempos of movement. Stay connected by maintaining eye contact and focusing on feeling him.

## Adapt Sex Positions Based on Your Response

Key in on your pleasure points and adapt sex positions and movements to stimulate your clitoris, G-Spot, or Deep Spot.

There are really only a handful of different positions, but modifying them in small ways can make a huge difference. For the purpose of keying in to what feels good, I would suggest that you limit other stimulation for the time being and just focus on what you can feel from intercourse.

## Clitoral Stimulation

The two best positions for stimulating the clitoris during intercourse hands-free are Woman on Top and Coital Alignment Technique. Focus on moving in a way that feels enjoyable to you.

Woman on Top will give you control of the position and movement to discover what feels good. To stimulate the clitoris when on top, you need to make contact with his pelvis by riding low. Your vulva should fully press against his body. To bring your clitoris into play even more, tip your pelvis forward or lean your whole body forward. This has the added benefit of putting your breasts into perfect position for fondling or sucking. Sometimes spreading your legs far apart to fully engage his body can strain your hips. Add a pillow under his bottom to elevate him. Think about feeling him and allowing him to feel you. Create the movement that feels good to your clitoris during manual stimulation. It may be up and down, or circles, or pulsing, side to side, or whatever works for you. Take your time and don't feel rushed.

Coital Alignment Technique is a variation of missionary position. With the woman on bottom, the man enters his wife. Instead of being up on all fours, he gently lays on her, resting his weight on his elbows. He then shifts his body up towards her head causing the shaft of his penis to rest across her vulva and clitoris. Rather than thrusting in and out with his penis, they gently rock, pushing back and forth. Engage your pelvis and Kegels to increase tension and build arousal. Direct his movements by placing your hands on his butt or hips.

During Coital Alignment Technique, some women like to have their legs lifted in order to fully engage their husband's body against theirs. Other women like to shift their legs to the inside of their husband's legs to more closely hug his penis. This variation allows women to stretch their legs to create tension. Some women enjoy the feeling of being fully pinned against the bed by not using a pillow under their head.

The movement to stimulate your clitoris will feel much less stimulating to your husband than thrusting does. If he is young, it will help him last longer. If he is older, you may need to assure him not to worry about his erection. You can always help him get it back. He needs to just relax and connect with you.

## G-Spot Stimulation

The three best positions for G-Spot stimulation are Woman on Top, Missionary, and Doggy Style. Remember the G-spot is located on the front wall of the vagina, only about an inch inside. It responds to firm pressure passing across it. During intercourse, the head of the penis must press into the front wall of the vagina. Move slowly enough that the penis might actually feel the bulging of the G-Spot.

To stimulate the G-Spot during Woman on Top, the woman must sit upright or even arch back to position the head of his penis across her front wall. Rather than riding him low, ride him high. With each stroke, slowly and firmly feel the head of his penis press into your G-Spot.

During Missionary Position, the wife needs to lift and rotate her hips up to force the penis to push across the G-spot during thrusting. With him kneeling between her legs, she can lift her legs over his shoulders or place her knees against his chest to elevate her bottom. She can also prop herself up on pillows or a wedge. Some men will hold the crook of her knees in his arms to elevate her while kneeling between her legs. The goal is concentrated energy against her G-Spot, so focus on shallow thrusting. Think about the speed and pace that feels good during manual stimulation of the G-Spot and emulate it.

The final position that works well to stimulate the G-spot is the doggy position. Because the wife has a lot of freedom in changing the angle of her hips and she can raise or lower herself with her arms, she can find just the right angle to hit the spot. The strength that a husband can move against the G-spot in doggy position is also a big plus.

G-spot is all about concentrated energy and feeling each other below skin level.

## Deep Spot Stimulation

The best positions for Deep Spot orgasms are Woman on Top and Missionary, but any position that lends itself to deep penetration fits the bill. Remember one of the keys to Deep Spot is waiting until the wife is highly aroused to help avoid hitting the cervix during deep thrusting.

It is no surprise that Woman on Top works well for Deep Spot stimulation. The wife can fine-tune the location of deep penetration to avoid hitting the cervix. A confident wife can enjoy the energy of full engagement during deep thrusting to drive the point home.

In the Missionary position, spreading the legs wide or lifting them will allow for full penetration. Movement for Deep Spot stimulation can range from a passionate pounding to a sensuous merging and pressing into each other's bodies. Focus on feeling the depth of each other's being.

Understanding our bodies and the pathways to enjoyment can help us tweak positions and movements so they lead to even greater pleasure during intercourse. Take control, slow down and see what you can discover.

## Focus on Connection, Not Just on Mechanics

Don't fall into the trap of believing that if he just lasted long enough, you would orgasm during intercourse. Some days he could thrust all night long and the only thing it would do is make you sore. Arousal does not come just from mechanics but from connection. If you aren't enjoying something, stop. Slow things down, reconnect, and do something else sexually together.

Connection can come from watching your bodies fit together and marveling at God's design. You can speak words to each other to say, "Hey, can you feel me", or, "Let me catch up." Listen to each other's breath and feel the excitement mount. Kiss with abandon when you feel like you can't get enough. When we smile and our husbands smile, we know we are connected. When your husband holds you with strength and looks into your soul, connection happens. Arousal depends on a lot more than friction, so figure out how to connect during intercourse.

*Together with your husband, brainstorm ideas to stay more connected during intercourse. Ask him how he knows if you are fully present during intercourse. How do you know if he is fully present?*

## Let Go and Let God

On my journey, I sometimes felt like I was trying so hard to have an orgasm during intercourse that I had both hands clenched and an iron jaw. Failure and disappointment sometimes resulted in me bursting into tears as I curled into a ball.

I distinctly remember one frustrating night of trying to make things work during intercourse. That night turned out to be a turning point. In tears, I told my husband, "I can't do this anymore," and he held me while I prayed. I told God that I was done trying to make things work and I just gave it to Him. I told God I would thank Him for every new experience I enjoyed with my husband, and that if I never experienced an orgasm during intercourse, I was good. We stopped worrying about orgasm and started enjoying what was happening.

Somehow releasing my expectations freed me up to discover new things each and every time we connected. Our sex life is not something that most of us pray about, but we probably should.

## Create a Plan B

Learning to orgasm or experience more pleasure during intercourse can feel frustrating if every time our husbands finish, sex automatically ends. Sex does not have to end because he finishes. There are other ways to finish. You can create a Plan B.

A Plan B prevents a pattern of disappointment that can become a self-fulfilling prophecy. More importantly, a Plan B will help the two of you stop worrying so you can actually connect during intercourse. Without a Plan B, you may spend your entire time thinking, *Am I going to make it? Am I going to make it? Am I going to make it?* At the same time, your husband might be thinking, *Am I going to last long enough? Am I going to last long enough? Am I going to last long enough?* And are you really connecting then, or are you just worrying?

In order to create a Plan B, you will need to have a hard conversation. Pick a time not fueled with emotions in a neutral location. Your husband may not even realize you sometimes feel frustrated after intercourse. Be gentle and say something like this:

"I don't know if you realize this, but for women, having an orgasm during intercourse isn't always easy. I really want to enjoy intercourse, but I don't always finish. Not because you don't last long enough, but just because my body is complicated. Instead of enjoying what we have, I find myself worrying about finishing. Could we figure out a way that I can finish even if you are done? That way we both can relax and enjoy sex more."

Come up with an easy way for you to finish when he might be getting sleepy. It might mean finishing yourself with your hands while he plays with your breasts. It might mean pulling out a vibrator to use together. He might want to use his hands or mouth on you. The key is not shutting yourself down because you didn't finish during intercourse. Give yourself the freedom to enjoy the new sensations you experience together without worrying about the finish line. It is not too much work, time, or trouble. You are absolutely worth it.

Tell your husband that you need him to ask you every single time after intercourse with absolute sincerity, "Can we keep going?" Then resist the tendency to shut yourself down. Remember there is no hierarchy of orgasms. Enjoy what God gives you, and see what else you can discover along the way.

*Talk to your husband about creating a Plan B. Affirm that you want to remove the pressure for both of you so that you can discover new things.*

## Train Yourself

Our bodies can learn new things, but sometimes it requires focused practice towards a specific goal.

My daughter plays the violin. When she had complicated passages to learn, she slowed them down enough that she could play the correct notes in the right rhythm. As her fingers learned the correct patterns, she slowly increased the tempo until the music sailed from her fingers.

If we have a specific desire during sex, then sometimes we can train our body. For instance, let's say that you come very close to experiencing orgasm in the Woman on Top position but you just don't quite get there. What if you decided to train your body to respond easier in that position? On your own, while in the woman on top position, you could imagine that you were having sex with your husband while manually stimulating your clitoris to orgasm. After doing the exercise several times, is it possible that your body would roll over into orgasm easier in the woman on top position during intercourse with your husband?

Consider how you can take small steps to connect pleasure with certain situations. Train your body to respond to what you want.

## Final Thoughts

Over the course of my marriage, intercourse has drastically changed from something I just endured to something that frustrated the heck out of me to something I crave—regardless of whether I reach orgasm.

More than any other sexual act, intercourse has stretched my husband and me to talk about really hard things. It has forced us to focus not just on mechanics but on connection. We have thrown out every preconceived idea of what intercourse looks like and created something that works for both of us. And we have grown enormously because of it, individually and as a couple.

Many of the changes have taken place because my husband was willing to let me figure out what works for me. The surprising thing is how much my husband has enjoyed it too—and not just because I am enjoying it. Somehow, we are much more relaxed and connected during intercourse and he senses the difference.

My husband and I are not even close to having everything figured out, and once in a while I still struggle with expectations or frustrations. Even though it did not start out this way, I now thoroughly look forward to intercourse. When we come together, I feel like our thoughts meld as one even above our own pleasure. My hope and desire are that someday we might be so in tune to each other that we don't even know who is leading and who is following. Don't give up and think that because you don't enjoy intercourse today, you won't enjoy it down the road. Consider the challenges of intercourse an opportunity for growth and just another way that God makes you into ONE.

## Action Items

1. Ask your husband if you can take control during intercourse to discover something new. In Woman on Top position, focus first on creating stimulation of your clitoris, then your G-Spot, and finally your Deep Spot.
2. Spend some time day dreaming about what amazing intercourse would look and feel like. Think about the steps needed to make it a reality.

CHAPTER 17

# Delights and Other Delicacies

OVER THE COURSE OF OUR MARRIAGE, Jim and I have had a lot of sex, especially since my awakening. The memories that stick in my mind are the creative encounters one of us has planned—dancing in our back porch until clothes started to come off, fun in a tent set up in the backyard on a warm summer night, and an invitation to come home for lunch complete with appetizers.

New experiences stretched us as we vulnerably shared ourselves and in essence "got naked" with each other. Jim and I have created amazing memories together that we can draw on when we hit a dry spell. In this passage talking about sex, Proverbs 5:15 says, "Drink water from your own cistern, running water from your own well."

God wants us to create a cistern, or reservoir, of memories to draw on. We can draw on delights and delicacies etched into our mind to create excitement. These memories are not just for the sake of variety and excitement, but as an intimate way to express ourselves. But yes, okay, they are for the fun and excitement too.

I want to share some different delights and delicacies to help you expand your idea of connection and to spur on your own creativity. Psalm 18:19 says, "He brought me out into a spacious place; he rescued me because he delighted in me." God wants us to live in spacious places. The possibilities between husband and wife are endless.

**Spend some time with your husband recalling some of your favorite memories of connecting with him and why they were special.**

## Manual Sex Positions

His left arm is under my head,
    and his right arm embraces me. (Song of Songs 2:6)

Many women describe orgasms from manual stimulation as the most physically intense. With fewer distractions than during intercourse, women can focus on what they feel and experience. Hands and fingers provide plenty of clitoral stimulation, and orgasms can top the charts.

Instead of feeling guilty that orgasms during intercourse don't feel as strong, wives can share the amazing experience of manual orgasms with their husband. How awesome it is for a husband to see and feel the intensity of her orgasm!

Letting your husband pleasure you though manual stimulation can range from connecting to intense. At times you can feel like you are letting him in on a secret hidden deep inside and shared for the first time. Other times manual stimulation can feel as if God has woven you together so your husband can feel the intensity of his love by serving you. Manual stimulation provides unique opportunities for pushing boundaries and experiencing the eroticism of hidden pleasures. Here are just a few ideas of the fun manual stimulation can provide.

## Woven Together

Many manual stimulation positions can feel awkward. Somehow it seems like the husband's hand is always in the wrong position. Tired wrists and weird angles can make it hard for a husband to get the hang of things. The Woven Together position feels both natural and connecting. Of course, smooth hands, lots of lube, and connected movements are a given.

To get in the Woven Together position, spoon with the wife in front, but with her hips rotated so she is lying more on her back. The husband can wrap one arm under her neck to gain access to her breasts. The upper arm wraps around her front with his palm gently resting on her mound. Basically, Woven Together puts his hand in the position where her hand would naturally fall. The wife can leave things to her husband or she can naturally intertwine her hand with his to provide some guidance. Gently turning her head will provide access for kissing and talking.

Woven Together is a position that feels natural to many women. It provides connection and warmth while giving the husband great access.

## Wrapped Up

A husband can suggest this position when his wife is tired and overloaded. With his steady words he convinces her that it is okay for her to sit back and just relax while he wraps her up in his strong arms.

To get into position, the husband sits upright against the headboard with his legs spread apart. With his back supported by pillows, he gently guides his wife to sit between his legs. Facing away and resting her back against his chest she can let go and relax into his body. Her body must tuck in close so that his hands can reach all the way to her vulva.

Wrapping his arms around her, he can gently stroke and warm up her body. His face can nuzzle her hair and neck taking in her scent. He can gently run his fingers up and down her arms, around her breasts, and down her sides to her thighs. Eventually one of his hands can rest on her mound as he leisurely strolls his fingers around her vulva. He can spend time just feeling her clitoris through stillness and slow movements as he warms her up.

As her body begins to relax, she can let her head rest along one of his shoulders. The closeness and security of this position can lead to a different kind of experience that may be much less physical and seeking, but much more relaxing and surrendering. As she experiences pleasure, she can feel her body melt into her husband's and breathe deeply to let out the last ounce of tension. She can let her head drop back, or she can turn and find his lips as her husband tenderly loves her.

## *Up Close and Personal*

A huge contrast exists between the experience of a woman touching a man and a man touching a woman. When a woman touches a man's penis, husband and wife watch what happens. The show demands their full attention until the fireworks fly.

But when a man touches a women's vulva, husband and wife visually disconnect from her body. He kisses her and embraces her, and secretly slips a hand between her legs. Nobody talks about it or looks, and they barely acknowledge what's happening besides the occasional uncomfortable attempt at guidance or direction. It is just some anonymous thing that happens between her legs, while the real attention is lavished in more acceptable places. There is no grand finale to eagerly watch or anticipate from her vulva; rather, they await subtle clues of ecstasy.

Contrary to what many of us believe, our bodies are amazing. Although changes during arousal for women are not as obvious as men, a careful student of his wife will notice engorgement, physical changes, and even changes in color. So maybe a husband ought to give manual stimulation up close and personal and give his wife a sensual play-by-play of the amazing show he sees and feels.

Tell your husband that you want him to know your body more intimately. Invite him to watch as he arouses you with his hands and takes you over the top. Set up soft lights, and warm the room to make yourself comfortable. Gently spread your legs as he kneels between them. He can take you in with his eyes as he works his magic. For variety, have him try a thumb or palm. Smile at him once in a while, voice your pleasure, and let him see all of you as he discovers your amazing body.

## Creative Places

Skirts work wonders to open up new possibilities. A late-night bonfire, parking to watch the sunset, or a night on the couch watching a movie can lead to unexpected delights. Get creative and make some memories. The possibilities for manual stimulation are endless.

# Oral Sex

> Blow on my garden,
>> that its fragrance may spread everywhere.
> Let my beloved come into his garden
>> and taste its choice fruits. (Song of Songs 4:16)

One of the most intimate ways you can allow your husband to "know you" is through oral sex. Your husband will see, feel, and even taste you in ways that he has never experienced before. If you surrender and allow yourself to receive from your husband, you can experience some of the most delicious orgasms possible.

Statistically, oral sex provides one of the most consistent ways for women to experience clitoral orgasms. The tongue—warm, wet, smooth, and completely void of rough spots—is an incredible instrument to create pleasure for our delicate parts. Not limited by the restriction of hinged joints like fingers, it possesses 360 degrees of movement and limitless possibilities. As an added bonus, using the mouth frees up his hands to stroke breasts, nipples, thighs, and even the G-Spot.

Most women's greatest challenge with oral sex is our minds. We wonder if oral sex is okay. Our minds constantly worry whether our husbands enjoy what they're doing. We struggle to just relax. So, before we talk about helpful techniques and fun positions, let me try to put your mind at ease.

## Mindset

Though God does not clearly address oral sex in the bible, many people think Song of Songs suggests they enjoy each other with their mouths. In verse 4:16 she says to him on their wedding night:

> Awake, north wind,
>   and come, south wind!
> Blow on my garden,
>   that its fragrance may spread everywhere.
> Let my beloved come into his garden
>   and taste its choice fruits.

Whether or not this passage alludes to oral sex, God neither clearly mandates or prohibits it. Oral sex is another gray area in the Bible where we must discern for ourselves what is beneficial for our marriage bed.

Don't just look at individual verses to decide about oral sex. Look at who God is and what He wants for us. Within the boundary of marriage, I believe He wants us to enjoy freedom as we selflessly love each other. Read Song of Songs as a whole and gain an appreciation for the sensuous smells, tastes, adoration, and abandon they enjoy. This couple lives a freedom that few of us allow ourselves. That is what God wants in marriage, and you get to decide exactly what that looks like.

If past experiences tainted your view of oral sex, you need to know that God is a God who can heal anything—even that. Don't hold onto baggage as an excuse for living in a very small world. Go after healing by praying with a friend, seeing a counselor, or talking to your husband. God wants us to live in wide open spaces and enjoy all that He has given us.

Many women are concerned that their husbands really don't want to be down there. We worry that we smell or taste bad. Show the same consideration you expect from your husband by slipping into the shower to freshen up before sex. Consider grooming by trimming, shaving, or waxing the area to create a different experience. Rather than worrying about whether your husband enjoys giving oral sex, ask him.

Most husbands love to give their wives oral sex because they can feel their wives' bodies much better than when they use their hands. When your husband tells you that he loves it, believe him. Then ask him to keep telling you, because most likely you will need to hear it on a regular basis before you believe it.

One of the challenges of receiving oral sex is just that, receiving. While our husbands don't seem to have any trouble lying back and relaxing, this does not come naturally to many of us. Our heads fill with what we ought to be doing or we worry about our husbands working so hard. We wonder if he has a crick in his neck or if we are taking too long. Don't give up just because he needs to shift positions. Just slide a pillow under your bottom or find a position that affords more comfort for him. Sex needs to be a balance of serving and receiving. Would you like it if your husband continually gave you gifts but would never receive a gift from you? Be a blessing to your husband by letting him serve you.

Some women struggle with the physical distance between the two of you during oral sex. The act can feel so intimate and intense that we feel as if we are on the edge of a cliff with nothing to hang onto. How your husband holds you can make a difference. Rather than focusing on just a single point of contact, create many points. Have him wrap an arm under your bottom to anchor you. Ask him to stroke your mound or torso to get the blood flowing. Maintain eye contact and watch him treasure you. Create points of connection to bridge the gap.

## Helpful Techniques

We create excitement and arousal through contrast. Playing with less sensitive areas generates a yearning for more focused stimulation. A warm still tongue pressed into the vulva makes our bodies ache for movement. Light feathery touches awaken our nerves and heighten sensation in anticipation of full encompassing strokes of connection. Great sex is composed of crescendos and decrescendos. The whispers contain as much power as the screams of exhilaration.

Most men don't intuitively understand the power of contrast. Their "go to" seems to be to dive right in and "get 'er done". More action, more pressure, more movement. Just keep going and something will happen. For us, the movement can almost feel dizzying and at best mechanical. If you crave connection from your husband, then you may need to have a talk. Think about the difference between rubbing and feeling.

This is the beginning of connection and is really just the tip of the iceberg.

One of the best instructional books to help men give their wives great oral sex is called *She Comes First*, by Ian Kerner. A secular book but respectfully written, the book literally details step-by-step instructions that any man can follow. More importantly, the book teaches important concepts like the power of stillness to create anticipation. Though we don't want our husbands to use a formula for oral sex, learning the basic steps of arousal and seeing their impact will help men move towards what their wives enjoy.

One way for your husband to learn what you like is by playing a game called "Rope a Dope." After your husband warms you up, he holds his mouth still on your vulva. Move your body against his mouth in order to create the stimulation you desire while he remains still. When you stop, his job is to imitate your movement. Then it is your turn again. The game will help you listen to your body and what it yearns for and will help your husband learn what you like.

Rhythms can help awaken our bodies by creating anticipation. For instance, a husband strokes three times almost to the clitoris, and the fourth time he just grazes over it. Then three times almost to the clitoris and the fourth time he just grazes over it. The rhythm entices our body to wake up and pay attention. The possibilities remain endless as we create anticipation through establishing rhythms.

Help your husband learn what great oral sex looks like for you. Communicate about what feels good and help him to slow down. Teach him the power of anticipation, creating contrasts, and intentional directionality. Show him what great oral sex looks like by doing it to him. Create a journey he never imagined, filled with twists and turns, and an intensity that only comes from connection.

## Oral Sex Positions

Besides the obvious position of lying on your back with your bottom propped up, here are a few ideas.

### 69

One of the most erotic oral sex positions for men can feel ultra-vulnerable for women. It requires an openness and exposure that rivals few other acts. With him on his back, straddle him on all fours with your face near his penis and your vulva near his mouth. Ask your husband to wrap his arms around you to hold you and help you feel secure. Also take advantage of the visual show that happens as your husband exposes himself.

### Lazy 69

This position provides simultaneous oral pleasure but can feel relaxing for both husband and wife while providing loads of skin-to-skin connection. Align your bodies similarly as you would for the traditional 69-position but lie on your sides in a gently curled up position. The wife will spread her knees apart so that the husband can rest his cheek on her inner thigh while she rests her head on a small pillow. Both husband and wife can gently pull the other closer for more intimate contact. Hands can freely stroke, caress, or grasp. If the wife wants more access to his testicles or perineum, she can gently spread his legs.

## Straddling His Face

When a wife feels absolutely at the peak of confidence and is thoroughly warmed up she can straddle her husband's face. Her body feels sleek, clean, and sexy, and she feels secure asking for what she wants. She knows her husband wants to give it to her. In fact, he doesn't just want to give it to her. It turns him on.

The wife might start out by giving her husband oral stimulation or manual stimulation with him lying on his back, his head propped up with a pillow so that he can see better. When she is ready, she can transition by telling him it is her turn. She can spend some time kissing, rubbing her body along his, and eventually make it clear that she has even bigger plans.

She can then move into position, straddling his face so he can pleasure her with oral stimulation. While she holds a headboard to provide support, a husband can provide additional connection and stimulation by using his hands on her buttocks or breasts. The wife can take control of the movement, pressure, and pace. She can fully open herself up and take advantage of building tension by flexing her pelvis forward as the husband gains full access to her body.

# Toys

> You are a garden locked up, my sister my bride:
> You are a spring enclosed, a sealed fountain.
> (Song of Songs 4:12)

Vibrators are quickly becoming more mainstream in our world, and many Christians wonder how they fit into God's design for sex. Available at in-home parties, drugstore shelves, and on websites, women buy vibrators because they work. Vibrators work because they produce a strong physical stimulation that makes the likelihood of orgasm for women higher, which can be a great thing.

However, we need to be careful about always using vibrators just because they work. As another gray area that the Bible does not specifically address, God calls us to discern with our spouse if using a vibrator could benefit our marriage. Consider the question, "Will using a vibrator create intimacy in our marriage?"

We need to remember that sex goes beyond just having the largest orgasm. God created sex as a way for us to connect, provide comfort, and get to know each other. But He also created sex as a way to grow each other by doing things like learning to use words to create arousal or tapping into creativity to express ourselves and turn each other on. If we always rely on physical stimulation, we will miss out on stretching in other ways of knowing each other. Defaulting to an easy route to the finish line can short-change us and our spouse.

I am not against vibrators. There are many cases where a vibrator can be an amazing tool. But we need to constantly ask ourselves, "Are we creating intimacy?" So, besides the obvious answer of using a vibrator to learn how to orgasm, I am going to share some examples where a vibrator might create intimacy.

## Orgasm During Intercourse

For the majority of women, orgasm does not come easily during intercourse, yet we have a deep desire to experience our bodies letting go while intertwined with our husbands. A vibrator used during intercourse can provide the additional clitoral stimulation needed to finish, and along the way it can provide pleasurable vibrations for our husbands.

If a wife is working toward enjoying intercourse more, she can also use a vibrator as an easy Plan B. Both husband and wife can just enjoy what happens during intercourse. If she doesn't reach orgasm before he does, then the vibrator can help her finish.

The vibrator can be a tool to help both spouses enjoy intercourse more. Will there be times when you might want to simplify and focus on what you can feel without the vibrations? You bet! Keep communication open, discern with God, and make no hard and fast rules.

## Day Off or Quickie

I have a husband who has always been thoughtful about making things enjoyable for me. But honestly, sometimes I think I am a lot of work. Wouldn't it be fun if sometimes our husbands could just enjoy sex and not worry about their wives so much? Maybe on the Sabbath, you treat your husband by letting him use a vibrator on you.

Seasons happen when life gets busy. We have young kids or crazy work schedules, and only a few minutes are available for leisurely connection. Rather than just always serving our husbands, we could also enjoy a quickie by breaking out the vibrator.

Sex ought to be about all kinds of experiences together, including effortless sex and quickies for two. They are new ways of getting to know each other. Could a vibrator create intimacy by tapping into a wider range of experiences? Would it create intimacy if you did it this way every time?

## Aging or Physical Challenges

I have had perfect eyesight my entire life. A few years ago, reading started becoming problematic. Honestly, for a while I avoided going down to my wood shop because I couldn't see the numbers on the tape measure. I was missing out on something that I loved. I finally hauled myself to the eye doctor to find out my options. It took some getting used to, and I still wish I had my young eyes, but I am adjusting to glasses and enjoying life again.

Vibrators can help both men and women as their bodies become less responsive due to age, medication, or some other physical challenge. It may take some getting used to the idea and you may grieve the loss of what you had, but using a vibrator can help people enjoy their sex life again.

Could vibrators create intimacy if they allowed a husband and wife to enjoy their sex life together, even when their bodies do not cooperate?

## Understanding Vibrators

One of the common concerns about vibrators is whether they make our bodies become less responsive to our husbands.

Our bodies are trainable. If you always use a vibrator, then your body will learn to respond to a vibrator. If you continue to have sex different ways, then your body will continue to respond to different experiences. If you have always used a vibrator and you want your body to respond in new ways, it will take time for your body to learn new things. If you get used to having an orgasm in five minutes with a vibrator, you will have to adjust to spending more time to respond. Understand how your body works and create the experience you want.

Asking the question, "Are we creating intimacy?" is not a one-time deal. We need to constantly ask and discern areas that we can stretch in experiencing each other. God created sex as a way to get to know each other. If you have never used a vibrator, then it could be a very intimate way to let your spouse know you. If you always use a vibrator, then there might be other ways to grow in connection that would more than compensate for less physical stimulation. Be discerning and ask the question, "Are we getting to know each other?"

## Breast Play

> May your breasts be like clusters of grapes on the vine.
> (Song of Songs 7:8)

Our husbands love our curves, especially our breasts. In fact, sometimes it feels like they are more interested in our breasts than in any other part of our body. Our breasts capture their eyes and entice their hands and fascinate them.

Many of us have baggage involving our breasts, whether we developed large breasts and constantly endured unwanted eyes or smaller breasts that caused us to feel insecure. Messages from society about our breasts have shaped how we feel and can limit how much we let ourselves enjoy breast play. Spend some time praying about the messages that have affected how you feel about your breasts and ask God to tell you what's true. You are fearfully and wonderfully made.

Our breasts are probably the most finicky part of our body. Hormones dramatically impact whether touch feels good or just plain old hurts. What can feel amazing one day can literally scream pain the next. Arousal levels also influence what touch we like. Help your husband understand the different touches that work and when they work. Communicate your needs patiently as he tries to navigate a terrain that constantly changes.

Breast play takes all shapes and forms, from the simple light touches where your breast meets your torso to firm pulling or twisting of the nipple during high arousal. Breast play alone can act as foreplay, take you all the way to orgasm, or act as the final push to the top during other stimulation. Breasts can be stimulated by hands, mouth, penis, testicles, and any other body part you can imagine.

Breast play can be a sensual and erotic experience for both the husband and the wife. You don't have to have large breasts, but you do have to have the confidence to share yourself. You also have to appreciate the erotic visual show that breasts create.

Breasts can be decorated with whipped cream to create a multisensory experience of taste, touch, and sight. Cover your breasts and let him enjoy dessert.

Larger breasts can be pulled together to form a wonderful chamber for his penis. Add lubrication for smooth sensual movement that will feel wonderful to him.

Regardless of the size of your breasts, you can enjoy stimulation of your nipples with the head of his penis. While a wife relaxes with her arms gently clasped above her head, a husband can straddle his wife's waist on his knees. Taking advantage of an amazing view, his hands can leisurely massage her sides, inside arms, and around the breasts to warm her up. Nipples can be teased with light accidental brushes of his hands as he makes his way from one side to the other. Every part of her body ought to be thoroughly relaxed except for the tension being slowly built where he fixes his eyes. Eventually he can gently massage the areola, the dark circle around the nipple, to further awaken the nipples.

When she is ready, the husband can slide up far enough for his penis to reach her nipples. While she watches, he can use his hand and his pelvis to gently push the head of his penis up and across her nipple. First one breast, and then the other. If she wants stronger pressure, she can take some lube and then use her hand to hold his penis against her nipple as he thrusts forward. If she wants additional stimulation on her clitoris, he can use his hand, or she can use hers.

This position is all about the view. He has a close-up view of the most sensitive part of his body joining with her mesmerizing breasts. He can watch her eyes as she abandons to pleasure. She has a close-up view of his manhood yearning for her while his eyes gaze on her breasts. She sees his face as he is overcome with pleasure.

Breasts are an amazing part of our body to create some fun. The real power comes when our excitement feeds on our husband's thrill. Breast play will call you to watch the show you create.

*Help your husband understand your breasts. Share with him what feels good and when. Come up with a signal to communicate when he needs to stay away or handle them with care.*

## Final Thoughts

> Let us go early to the vineyards
>   to see if the vines have budded,
> if their blossoms have opened,
>   and if the pomegranates are in bloom—
>   there I will give you my love.
> (Song of Songs 7:12)

I used to think my husband needed creativity in the marriage bed. I thought I needed to dress up, surprise him in new locations, or come up with a new move. It weighed me down and made me feel inadequate. Honestly, I don't think my husband really cared that much. I now understand that creativity in the marriage bed is something that I need. Women are the ones with 50 pairs of shoes, not our husbands.

Culture has taught us to sit back and wait for our husbands to lead in the marriage bed, yet in Song of Songs, she is the one who initiates a little outdoor adventure. She plans a rendezvous early in the morning out in the vineyards to give him her love.

Sharing our creativity with our husband takes courage. We take the risk that to surprise our husbands may result in rejection. We may catch him in the wrong mood, create embarrassment, or get a less than enthusiastic response. You might plan something and enjoy an amazing evening together and still wake up the next morning wracked with insecurities, thinking, "Oh my gosh, what did I do?"

I would rather live than plod through life. I would rather feel both the sting of rejection and the exhilaration of connec-

tion than the numbness of a safe life. God filled me with creative ideas of how to connect with my husband. It has required
me to ground myself in knowing that I am God's Beloved,
wonderfully complex, unique, and exactly like He wants. I
know that God wants me to keep sharing myself regardless of
the reception. God calls me share my creative energy with
Jim.

## Action Items

1. Talk with your husband through some of the different
   ideas in this chapter and generate a list of your own.
2. Take some time to daydream about an encounter you
   would like to create with your husband. Then have the
   courage to plan it.

# CHAPTER 18

# Feeling Wanted

IT WAS ANOTHER LONG NIGHT of tossing and turning. Jim had reached for me, and I had turned him down—not for the reasons you would guess. I had turned him down because I didn't want pity sex. I didn't want him to initiate just because he knew it had been too long. I wanted him to want me, to desire me, to not be able to keep his hands off me. Now maybe that sounds romantic and unrealistic, but don't we all deep down want to be desired?

After my sexual awakening, my husband and I switched roles, and I became the higher-drive spouse. All of a sudden, I understood how he had felt when I wasn't all that interested in sex. Rarely did I experience the sting of rejection, but even having a spouse who doesn't clamor to initiate before you do can feel like rejection. At the heart of it, we don't just want to have sex a certain number of times per week. We want to feel desired.

Couples probably argue about how often to have sex as much as anything else. Initially, increasing the frequency may improve the situation. Eventually, though, most people realize that's not the real issue. *Who wants to constantly pursue and never be chased?*

How often we have sex—one of the most measurable gauges of our sex life—only scratches the surface of marriage dynamics. Just as important are the topics of who initiates and when, and who takes the lead.

Underneath it all, both wives and husbands want to feel desired. As we build trust in marriage and we learn the truth about sex, we can go beyond playing control games during initiation and instead give ourselves to each other. Ultimately, as wives learn to let go of control, we can encourage our husbands in the role God gave them, to lead.

## Frequency

Many couples ask, "How often should we have sex?"

The higher-drive spouse fishes for evidence to up the ante, while the lower-drive spouse looks for ammunition to sabotage any advances. We try to validate our own needs to encourage our spouse to change. Most counselors advise couples to compromise and find some middle ground. For example, if he wants to have sex seven times a week and you want it once a week, you can agree to having sex three times a week. But isn't that just buying into what the world believes about sex, that it is just a physical urge driven by hormones? This view says that if I feel like having sex, then we should have sex, or if I don't feel like having sex, then I don't need sex. But what if our drive doesn't have anything to do with how often we should have sex?

The whole frequency discussion changes when we understand God's design for sex. Rather than letting our hormones control us, we embrace God's design for sex to transform our marriages. We reach for our husbands when we feel disconnected or misunderstood. When stress burdens our husbands, we help release their tension and affirm that we're there for them. When the kids drive us crazy, we escape together to refresh. We have sex because we need it, because our husbands need it, and because our marriages cannot thrive without it.

When we understand God's design for sex, doesn't the answer to "How often should we have sex?" become, "How intimate do you want your marriage to be?"

Jim and I have gone through different periods in our life. When we first got married, everything was new and exciting, and we had lots to learn. Enjoying sex often probably helped us more than we realized as we adjusted to marriage. After the kids came, life got busy. Sex happened less and less. I gradually became the gatekeeper. Even though we got along, we were distant.

Since my awakening, sex has taken on a whole new meaning and created intimacy at a whole new level. Even though I no longer have a sex drive, I crave connection with my husband. We have sex often, and I cannot imagine ever going back, but sometimes we still must intentionally make time.

# Intentional Craving

Intentionally connecting in marriage is really no different than being intentional in our relationship with God. When I drift away from God, I make intentional decisions to create connection. I spend time in His Word, praying, and just worshipping Him. In the beginning, carving out time takes a conscious effort. As I spend more and more time with God, I look forward to and even crave more time with Him. Eventually I get to this sweet spot where I am so connected with God that if I miss a day I notice.

Isn't that where we want to get with our husbands? To a sweet spot so intimate that when we drift apart things feel off? If we haven't had sex for a while, we feel out of sorts. Rather than our drive determining when we have sex, our need for connection does.

A lot of our differences in drive might disappear if we expanded our definition of sex. The other day I was visiting with a mom of three young kids. Even though she understands the importance of sex, simple exhaustion has left her with little motivation to connect.

She knew that her husband hoped for sex three times a week, but she could not fathom it. I encouraged her to think outside the box. I said, "What if you and your husband had an agreement that four times a week the two of you would climb into bed naked for at least 30 minutes? Two of those times, you would do your best to engage in sex, but the other two times you would come with no expectations besides connecting skin to skin. You could enjoy backrubs, cuddling, talking, or whatever." All of a sudden, her eyes lit up and she said,

"That sounds great!" Opening up the definition of sex to include simply lying skin to skin changed everything for her.

Most couples have sex at 11 pm, which is probably the worst time of day. Planning different times to connect can make a huge difference. That might mean a morning shower together, having the kids fix their own breakfast and watch cartoons, hopping in bed as soon as the kids go to bed, hiring the sitter to take the kids out, or creating a sacred Sunday afternoon where you lock yourselves in the room for a nap.

You might worry that if you devote all this time to your marriage your kids will suffer. The truth is, as you take time for yourselves and intimately connect, your outlook on life will change. Your being happy and connected will do more to make your kids happy and grounded than any activity to which you could cart them. Make intentional decisions to create the intimate marriage that God wants for you.

When women choose to learn about godly sexuality in an Awaken-Love class or another study, they prioritize intimacy with their husbands. As they read articles, do homework, and talk with their husbands about what they are learning, they start to awaken. They begin expressing themselves, sharing creative ideas, and focusing on connection rather than orgasm. Women are often shocked by how much they look forward to sex when real connection happens on a regular basis.

*Have a conversation with your husband about ways the two of you can prioritize sex. Share with him ways that he can help you prioritize intimacy and ask how you can help him.*

# Desire Follows Arousal

Most women don't have a drive like a man; our drive follows arousal. In other words, we won't feel like having sex until we are in the middle of making love. That doesn't mean we don't need sex or won't enjoy it. We just have to give our husbands a chance to get us in the mood.

Also, the longer women go without sex, the less we care about it and the harder it is for us to respond. When Jim and I went weeks without intimately connecting, I could have cared less about having sex and would have told you I didn't need it either. When I did finally agree to sex, it took Jim forever to warm me up. I remember feeling nervous and anxious just getting naked with my husband

Thankfully, the inverse is also true. The more I have sex, the more I want it and the easier it is for me to respond. I did not start making real progress in terms of responsiveness, communication, and connection until we were making love on a regular basis.

Only you and your husband can decide what works for you—but if you want sex to get easier and better, then you need to have it often. Try an experiment to find out just what a difference regular physical connection makes. Decide on a predetermined goal of 30-60 days in a row. Talk to your husband and intentionally make plans so that you can succeed. Discover just how intimate your marriage can be when you let God glue you together through sex.

One woman shared that although she and her husband already had a good sex life, once they began having sex every day, if they missed even one day, she missed sex. As the old saying goes, "Maybe you don't know what you're missing if you've never had it." If you want sex to improve, you need to commit to regular connection.

## Initiating

Initiating sex requires courage and security in who God created you to be. We risk rejection by asking our spouse to accept us and enter into our world. Initiating sex exposes the core of our being. If you think it's no big deal, then you have never experienced sexual rejection yourself. Until I became the higher-drive spouse, I had no idea how much hurt I had carelessly inflicted on my husband.

Initiating sex can become a huge area of conflict in marriage. Wounds build, and we grasp for control in order to protect ourselves. My marriage pastor once taught, "Men crave intimacy, but they settle for control." Initiating sex can easily become a battle for control rather than an expression of intimacy.

In some marriages, the wife decides she should never say no to her husband. What started as a biblical choice turns into resentment as she feels like she has lost all power over her own body. Even though her husband may initially feel like he has a sweet deal, eventually things just turn sour because he really wants her to say "yes"—and if she can't say "no," then how can she ever really say "yes"?

In other marriages, past experiences or struggles with porn have created a fear of intimacy, causing the husband to control everything about initiation. Sex happens on his terms, in the middle of the night and as quickly as possible. Sex boils down to a physical urge that he must get rid of when no one can see.

In many marriages, the husband may initiate sex, but *we* control what happens. We open the gate when sex feels convenient to us, or when our hormones surge, or when we start feeling guilty because we haven't made love in a while. Meanwhile, our husbands patiently wait, looking for our signal, wondering if we're in the mood. They have learned that unless sex happens on our timetable, rejection will most likely follow.

What initially seems like a healthy thing—a sensitive husband working around his wife's needs—can soon turn into timidity, which is a total turn-off for us. As we gain an understanding of God's design for sex and release the lies and baggage, we need to step into God's design for mutuality with sex.

> 1 Corinthians 7:3-5 says:
> The husband should fulfill his marital duty to his wife, and likewise the wife to her husband. The wife does not have authority over her own body but yields it to her husband. In the same way, the husband does not have authority over his own body but yields it to his wife. Do not deprive each other except perhaps by mutual consent and for a time, so that you may devote yourselves to prayer. Then come together again so that Satan will not tempt you because of your lack of self-control.

I have to be honest. This has never been my favorite scripture passage about sex. It makes me feel like a piece of meat created to fulfill my husband's physical urges. People use these verses to guilt wives into having sex with their husbands. Fortunately, we know that God does not want us to just operate out of obligation. God wants us to operate out of an outpouring of an abundance of love. God wants your heart, not just your actions, and so does your husband.

This verse does not say, "A husband has authority over his wife's body." It says, "She yields it to her husband." We have authority over our own bodies, and when we establish trust and appreciate the power of sex, then we yield to our husbands as they yield to us. We stop using sex as a way to control each other and learn to both give and receive from each other. We stop demanding that our spouses only initiate on our timetable and we have the freedom to initiate when we want to make love.

It is not just that our bodies are not our own, it is that our spouses' bodies are ours—not because we own them, but because their wholeness is as important as our own. We know when they feel weary, discouraged, or under attack. We know when to reach out and when to just hold their hands. It is not just about fulfilling each other's physical needs, but about being one. Through the mystery of oneness, we can love each other better.

Nobody can make you give up authority of your body—not God, not your pastor, and not your husband. It is something that we do as we gain trust with our husbands and see their humanness in contrast to our God that steadies us. Ultimately, giving up authority is our choice.

What God is calling us to is radical. Giving yourself to your spouse—mind, body and soul—is the most terrifying thing you will ever do. When we initiate, we give ourselves to our spouse, saying, "Come, and join me." When we accept their advances, we trust that our spouse cares as much about us as they do about themselves. To give ourselves freely can only happen when we are grounded in God.

## Leading

Women want their husbands to lead. We want them to lead spiritually, to lead the family, and to lead in the marriage bed. We want strong confident lovers who know how to hold us and give us what we need, even when we don't know ourselves. Even though we want these things, most women are pretty terrible at letting their husbands lead—in the marriage bed or anywhere else.

When my husband used to plan a date, I always had a better idea. We'd get in the car and I'd ask, "So, where are we going tonight?" And he'd say, "I was thinking that new little Mexican restaurant down the street, and then catch the latest episode of Star Wars." Already my wheels were spinning, thinking about what *I* wanted. "Hmmm, I'd really rather go to _____", and my kind husband would shift plans because he wanted to make me happy.

Pretty soon, I was bemoaning the fact that my husband couldn't plan anything. "Why do I have to make all of the decisions? Can't he just plan something?" I thought.

Women always seem to have a better idea, don't we? Whether that's the route we take to church or the flavor of ice cream we buy, we certainly have a lot of opinions about how things should be done. When our husbands clean or take care of the kids, we let them know the "right" way to do it. Pretty soon, our husbands hardly know how to make a decision on their own!

If we want our husbands to become the leaders of our families, we have to start by demonstrating that we trust them, even in the smallest of decisions. For me, this meant asking Jim's forgiveness and then committing to letting go of control, starting with the small, daily decisions. If I can't trust my husband to choose a parking space, how can I trust him to lead our family or to lead me in our marriage bed?

I have a theory that few wives *actually* let their husbands initiate sex. We might think they do, but most of us have trained them to wait until we give them some subtle signal that we are open to sex. We might wear a certain outfit to bed, linger when we touch, or drag them to bed early. Ultimately, *we* decide when we have sex.

If we want our husbands to lead, we need to let them lead, even in the marriage bed. After my awakening, I realized I wanted my husband to have permission to initiate, even when it was not on my mind or agenda. If he needed to feel loved, or if he felt disconnected, or he just wanted sex, I was in.

After 20 years of training him to wait for my signal, things did not change easily. In order to break the pattern, we came up with a plan. I would have 48 hours to initiate. Once we'd made love then he would have 48 hours, and we would just keep taking turns. We assured each other that even if sex wasn't on our minds, we would get ourselves on board.

I worried that my husband might feel controlled, but he said he found our plan really freeing. Instead of constantly trying to figure out if that was my signal or if it was a good time, he could simply initiate whenever he wanted to. He looked forward to his turn to make plans for us.

It only took a few weeks to break our old pattern. What an amazing thing for my husband to plan dates and initiate sex because he wanted to make love to me!

Leading a woman in the marriage bed is pretty much a nightmare. We have all these romantic ideas, yet we have a hard time letting go of control and just relaxing. After tiptoeing around in order to make us happy, many husbands start getting timid—which is the opposite of what turns us on!

I want to share some specific things that you can do to encourage your husbands to lead.

***Ask you husband what you need to let go of control of so that he can lead.***

## Expand His Repertoire

Your husband needs a huge repertoire of delights and delicacies so that he can adjust to meet your needs in different situations. You have to show your husband different things that you might like. Manual sex can feel very different depending on whether you are in the position of Wrapped Up, Woven Together, or Up Close and Personal. Help him expand his repertoire by showing him different techniques and positions to hold you, touch you, and connect with you.

## Express Emotions

Help your husband learn to hold you in different ways based on how you feel. When you feel sad, you might say, "I just need you to cover me tonight." When you feel insecure, teach him how to maintain a firm touch and ask him not to let go of you. Treat him to sex when you feel playful by wrestling and teasing. As you show your husband how to play out emotions during sex, he will learn to make love in different ways.

## Take Your Turn

One of the best ways to show your husband what it means to lead is to take the lead yourself. Surprise him like you would want to be surprised. Tease him like you would want to be teased. Take charge, have a plan, assure him that you've got this and then do it like you mean it. Spend time afterward talking through why it was so hot for you and what you would love him to do sometime.

## Give Him Ideas and Permission

If you have specific ideas of a sex scenario that you would like to play out, you may need to have a conversation with your husband in advance. In fact, you might need to have several conversations in order to communicate what you want and that you really want it. A loving husband who has spent his life being kind, considerate, and gentle may take a little convincing that you really want to be taken. If it turns you on to have your husband take you to the wall or splay you out while holding your hands above your head, or ask you to watch, then you might have to communicate why. What does this represent to you? Why does it turn you on? Communicate your trust and your desire to fully surrender to him.

## Let Him Off the Hook

Our bodies are finicky depending on the time of month, how our day went, how many kids slobbered on us, or our insecurity for the day. Our husbands can start to feel more and more unsure of themselves, which makes us feel even worse. Reassure your husband that he is not doing anything wrong; you're just having trouble. Ask him to help you get back on board by not giving up on you and instead try a different path.

## Affirm your Husband

Affirm your husband when he discovers something new about you or becomes bolder with his words. When he notices something you don't like, tries another path, or tries something new, let him know you noticed. As he becomes more confident and resilient in adapting to the situation, encourage him. Affirm him when you sense he is more present and connected to you. The best thing you can do to influence growth in your husband is to encourage him in every small step he takes in the right direction.

# Final Thoughts

I am going to be really vulnerable and tell you that I have a terrible time letting my husband lead. Whether in the day-to-day decisions of where we go on a date, facilitating a small group, or in bed, I am much more comfortable taking charge than following. To enjoy something that I did not choose takes a concerted effort. I have to literally pause, take a deep breath, tell myself to relax, and sometimes pray for God's help.

Letting go of control with our husbands helps us learn how to let go of control with God. When we do all the talking and make all the plans, we miss out on what God has for us. As I have made a concerted effort to let Jim lead, I've watched him grow in confidence, both in the bedroom and out of the bedroom. Rather than always asking what I want to do, he shares the fun of planning dates.

For our 29th anniversary, Jim planned a surprise overnight on a bed and breakfast train in Wisconsin! It was an old train with narrow aisles, and when we saw our room we just busted up laughing.

Our beds were two tiny bunk beds along the window. The bathroom was so small that the sink tipped out of the wall above the toilet. We could not pass by each other without one of us sitting on the bed.

My resourceful husband had smuggled a bottle of red wine on board and two small plastic wine cups, so we quickly closed our door and sat down for a little foot rub before dinner.

At 6:00 pm the train started a slow trek to view the leaves. The ride would only last three hours, and then the rest of the night we'd spend parked at the station as we enjoyed the amenities on board. The scenery was beautiful as dinner was served, but we were very aware the clock was ticking. Once the sun went down we had some private exploring to do while the motion of the train created a new dimension for connection.

We skipped dessert and zipped back to our room, past senior citizen after senior citizen who probably figured twin berths was not a bad way to go. We had to practically hop on one foot to strip down and tumbled into bed laughing all the way. Things were cozy, but as the darkness whirred by and the gentle jostling of the old tracks tossed us around, we were suspended in time. We slid easily into sleep after so much fun.

In the old days, I might have been really hard on my husband for booking a room with two tiny bunk beds for our anniversary. But honestly, this was one of the most fun trips we have taken. We laughed and laughed, and we marked something off of our bucket list that everyone ought to experience at least once in a lifetime—sex on a moving train! I would have missed out on an amazing memory-making adventure if we always did things my way.

## Action Items

1. Spend some time thinking about what it means for your husband to lead. What can you change about yourself in order to encourage him?
2. Lead during sex. I mean really lead, like you mean it. Show your husband what leading in the bedroom looks like and have some fun.

# CHAPTER 19

# Changing the World

"DOES ANYONE ELSE HERE FEEL ANGRY!?" It wasn't the first time I had heard it during class. When women realize how wrong they've been about sex, they get angry. Some feel betrayed or let down by the important people in their lives for not talking about sex. Others feel angry at the church for purity messages that set them up for failure or that always slanted sex towards the needs of men. Some realize how much baggage they've carried because sex outside of marriage was treated like the unpardonable sin. A few women wonder how they could have understood so little about their own bodies. Others hate how culture has shaped what they believed about their husband. Most of us have something to feel angry about involving our sexuality.

When righteous anger boils up, it moves us to action. I will never forget the fear of teaching my first classes. Regardless of how crazy or uncomfortable it felt, I knew I had to do *something*! Reading a book about sex may help you personally, but until you have the courage to engage in conversations face to face with others, our world does not change.

When we open up conversation with our kids, with no question off limits, we help them navigate our culture. As we create a marriage where sexual connection fuels fun, intimacy, and unity, our kids look forward to their own marriages. Churches that talk about real issues and real struggles create safe places for truth, healing, and wholeness. Our kids don't have to go through the same struggles that we did. We have the power to change the world—one daughter, one friend, one woman at a time.

As our kids and grandkids face greater challenges in the coming years surrounding sexuality, we could easily feel discouraged. If we were messed up by a lack of good information or our neighbor's Playboy magazine, how will this next generation survive a hook-up culture and internet porn?

It would be easy to throw our arms up and say, "What can we do?" Because honestly, porn is not going away. Culture will continue to use sex to sell everything from cars to alcohol. Morals continue to fall further and further from traditional Judeo-Christian values. Our kids face confusing choices about gender identity and sexual orientation. No longer is the scandal about who got pregnant or lost their virginity. Although the sexual revolution argued equal rights for women, little real progress has been made. Many wives continue to have unfulfilling sex lives, and the #metoo campaign has highlighted just how much sexual harassment and abuse continue.

Maybe the challenges we face are exactly the incentive we need to make real changes. We cannot change culture, but we can change the way we address sex. The blatant sexualization of our world is an opportunity to break open a topic that the church has skirted around for centuries because of fear. We can no longer afford to be silent.

Wives who watch a husband's constant battle with porn understand the importance for change. They strive to create open communication with their kids about sex from a young age. Husbands who fell into the trap of using women for sex want their kids to know that real satisfaction comes only from true intimacy. Women who resented their husband's sexual desire want their daughters to grow up looking forward to sex in marriage. Dads who spent years hiding in shame after they found porn, desperately want to spare their kids. They understand the importance of creating a safe place to talk about sex. We can change things.

Our kids do not have to grow up with the same messages that we received about sex. We can create a safe comfortable environment where our kids know that they can ask anything. Rather than just focusing on purity, the church can speak about the importance of living with sexual integrity. We can create safe communities for healing and encouragement.

## Talking to Our Kids

The women I know who stayed pure until marriage and easily transitioned to enjoying sex in marriage couldn't remember one specific talk with their parents about sex. From an early age, their parents educated them about their bodies, answered questions, and never made them feel embarrassed. As girls, they felt safe sharing their own struggles or even seeking advice for a friend. Conversations felt comfortable, respectful, and without limits. These parents didn't just talk about the importance of sex in marriage; they lived it. They made their marriage a priority and freely enjoyed intimacy as a way to strengthen their marriage. Our words will mean nothing if we don't believe it ourselves.

The sooner we open up conversations with our kids about sex, the better. If we avoid or dismiss our curious young kids, by the time they reach puberty we will be the last person they want to talk to. When my kids were young, we read a storybook called *How Babies Are Made* by Stephen Schepp. Reading about the details of sex felt as natural as learning how trees grow. Reading a book that used the proper terms for body parts helped me mask my discomfort I still had about the topic.

When we think about talking to our kids about sex, we typically think in terms of the nuts and bolts of making babies. But if you think about how many times you've had sex in your marriage, very few involve making babies. We have sex for many reasons, including connection, pleasure, comfort, and oneness. As you embrace opportunities to talk about sex, focus more on what God does to strengthen marriage through sex than on how to make babies.

Don't just create special dates to talk about sex, but embrace every opportunity to speak the truth—from young toddlers asking questions about their bodies to teenagers navigating technology. When situations in movies portray lies about sex, share what you believe about sex and why. Don't be afraid to share your own failures when appropriate.

Admit when you don't know the answer, but hang onto what God clearly tells us. Rather than pretending everything in the Bible is black and white, encourage your kids to involve God in their decisions. For instance, the Bible does not specifically address masturbation. However, it does teach very clearly about not letting something become our god or control us. The Bible also warns us over and over against lust. Share how lust impacted you and what you've learned. God also created us for relationship. If something fills you with shame and drives you into hiding, it creates separation. Help teenagers to talk through issues with you and encourage them to pray about what would please God.

Every conversation must start with some kind of affirmation like, "It's good to understand your own body", or, "Thank you for having the courage to talk to me." Every conversation should finish with a reminder like, "I am so glad you talked to me. You can always talk to me about anything." More than the actual conversation, your kids will remember your attitude about the conversation. If you cannot even talk to your husband about sex, how will you comfortably talk to your kids? You want to create a safe environment so if your child has seen something that makes them feel uncomfortable they will talk to you. When your daughter has hard choices, she needs to know that she can process them with you. We want to empower our kids and be a resource for them as they navigate a very complicated world.

When I was 14, I went on my first date with a 17-year-old. I didn't know him well but felt pressured into a double date by my friend. Though a double date might sound safe, it left me few options. As my friend and her boyfriend made out in the backseat, I endured touching and groping because I simply did not feel equipped to say "no."

We must instill self-respect within our daughters so they will feel empowered to make good choices and be prepared to address hard situations. Our girls need to know that God created sex as a beautiful way to mutually love each other in marriage. It is not a commodity for keeping a boyfriend or to stay popular.

We must create safe places for our sons to share the challenges they face in living a life of sexual integrity. We can teach them to respect, honor, and cherish girls with their words and with their eyes. They must understand God's beautiful design for sex in marriage.

Today's kids face choices and decisions that we never imagined. A wealth of information is available at their fingertips and can act as both a curse and a blessing. If you don't want your 5th grader to Google, "blow job", then he must feel safe enough to ask you what it means. Could you comfortably share enough information to handle conversations with his peers? When your high schooler shares about friends having anal sex, could you help her find information that might help her friends? Rather than ignoring the challenges of living in singleness into the late 20s, could you become a safe place for your grown kids to wrestle with how to live with sexual integrity?

Our kids need our help. The silence and awkward sex talks that we endured leave them swimming in dark murky waters without a life preserver. We must create a safe place for our kids to ask questions, seek advice, and wrestle with what they believe. We must share why God created sex and how it strengthens marriage. More than anything our kids need to see intimate marriages built on honesty, integrity, and a life dependent on God.

*Discuss with your husband how you can open up conversations with your kids about sex. With young kids you could read them some books. With school age kids you might start by simply asking, "What do the kids at school say about sex?" With teenagers, look for opportunities to talk about what it means to live with sexual integrity. Don't just talk about how babies are made. Talk about God's design for sex.*

## Talking about Sex at Church

A year after I started teaching classes to women in my back porch, word started getting back to the leaders at my church. Couples with huge smiles on their faces shared how much classes improved their marriage. Eventually the leaders asked if they could host Awaken-Love classes in the building.

When I teach wives, I try to advertise exclusively to women. The last thing I want is a husband poking his wife saying, "You should sign up for that!" One of my favorite marketing strategies was to hang fliers in women's bathroom stalls. I don't shy away from using the word "sex" because I want women to know what they are getting into. God created sex, and we don't have to disguise it as "intimacy."

One day at church I noticed all my fliers missing from the bathroom stalls. A 5-year-old had asked her mom, "What is sex?" after seeing my flier. Upset at having to address the question with her daughter, the mom met with trustees to voice her objection.

I understand a mom wanting to address sex on her terms, but she missed a wonderful opportunity. What better situation could you create than to have a child asking her *mom* about sex at *church*? The mom could have simply answered, "Sex is a way that God created for husbands and wives to love each other." Instead, I'm guessing the young girl immediately picked up on her mom's discomfort and fear about the topic of sex. Next time, her daughter will probably look for answers somewhere else.

The church's silence and discomfort communicate as much about sex as any sermon. Premarital counseling that dodges the topic or provides few real answers does as much harm as good. Accountability groups that secretly shuffle off to the back room create shame. Ignoring real issues of healing for men or women who have suffered abuse denies God's power. Teachings about purity without the reminder of God's grace and mercy totally miss the message of the gospel. Jesus came to save us all. We treat sex as if it is the untouchable sin—too big for God if you mess up, and if you do, your life will be doomed and your marriage ruined. Have we forgotten who God is?

Part of the reason so much transformation happens in Awaken-Love classes is because we meet in community. In six short weeks, we go from complete strangers to intimate friends determined to see the culture of sex changed for ourselves, our kids, and the next generation. We bond through our common stories and spur each other on as we witness God's transformation. Getting comfortable talking about sex in class rolls over into great conversations with our husbands, kids and friends.

On baggage week, women become sisters. They take turns sharing what has impacted their marriage bed and how God has shown up. The women gently honor each other's stories as they listen and pass the Kleenex box. Some share only what they are ready. Others fully embrace the opportunity to unpack years of shame. We pray together, weep, and call out the best in each other. Righteous anger boils up as women commit to changing sex for the next generation.

We have to create a culture of authenticity in church. Our buildings ought to be filled with broken people looking for transformation. When we create a safe place, we set God free to do what He does best. God can bring wholeness to our sexuality, but we must first bring it to the light.

If you want to continue strengthening your sex life or are looking for a great resource to bring up the topic at your church or with friends, consider hosting an Awaken-Love video class. You can find more information at **www.awaken-love.net.**

*Talking Point: How is God calling you to start speaking about sex in your church community? Pray about your next steps and talk through ideas with your friends.*

## Integrity vs. Purity

Many of us in the church grew up with strong messages of purity. Though well intended, the message sometimes felt manipulative and set us up for failure. Purity was this all-or-nothing concept. You either had it or you didn't. It was black or white. Once we crossed lines, whether by our choice or someone else's, we were ruined for life. We had lost our purity, so we gave up and spun out of control.

Purity was what you talked about in a high school youth group, but by the time you reached the average age that people get married (27), purity didn't hold much meaning.

Rather than purity, we need to teach about sexual integrity. Living with honesty and transparency, we strive to integrate God into all of our life, including our sexuality. We make the choice to live with sexual integrity every day, whether single or married, whether we have made many mistakes or few, whether we are divorced or widowed.

As singles we understand that God created the physical act of sex for marriage, but we also understand that He made us sexual beings from birth. Our sexuality drives us toward relationships and community with others and with God. We strive to care for our body and soul in all aspects.

In marriage we strive to care for ourselves but also for our relationship. Faithfulness to our spouse, connection, and undivided devotion ground our marriage. Sexual integrity calls us to openness and transparency with our spouse about everything.

Living with sexual integrity requires that we integrate God into our sex life. Decisions require openness, prayer, and discernment regardless of our situation. If we ask God, He will give us answers. Are you willing to surrender even your sexuality to Jesus?

Many people agree that the church needs to do a better job talking about sex, but how that happens has no easy answer. After my church's sermon series about the "sex talk," many people were thankful; others literally left the church. Although our pastors have a great influence, countless times I have witnessed real ministry taking place one-on-one as women mentor women, have lunch, and encourage and pray for each other. We do not have to wait for our pastors to lead the charge on addressing sex. That's part of the reason Awaken-Love is so effective. When we meet in homes, no pastor has to endorse the specifics of the class. We have the freedom to fully address topics and to provide real and respectful answers.

We can minister to each other and train each other up, which is something we probably should have done all along. Start sharing your testimonies of God's healing of sexual abuse or baggage, and people will discover a God who loves even their most vulnerable parts. Openly share your battle with lust or porn, and you will begin living a life of sexual integrity. Take away the power Satan holds by bringing your struggle into the light. Teach about the ways God connects husband and wife through sex, and you open up a window into real intimacy. Provide real answers, and you open the door for others to create an amazing sex life. God created sex, and it's time to take it back from the world. You are the church.

## Figuring It Out Ourselves

We start changing the world by changing ourselves. If you talk to your kids about sex, when deep down you still feel shame, your words will sound like a clanging symbol. If you lead a marriage class at church and you continue to emphasize the importance of sex for husbands, then you speak only half of the truth. When you tiptoe around brokenness like porn, the hook-up culture, or erotica, you reinforce the idea that

God cannot heal "that". Your actions speak louder than your words.

Before we can minister to others, we must understand the depth of God's love for us. We cannot communicate God's amazing design for sex in marriage until we experience the healing and restoration of our husbands taking us into their arms. Before we can communicate God's healing power, we must experience transformation in our own lives. We cannot create a safe place for others to be known until we understand the freedom of being fully known.

I often notice the visible changes of women set free. Free to be known. Free to fail. Free to live. We are a testimony to God's redeeming power in our lives. Our marriages are a testimony to the intimacy that two people surrendered to Christ can experience. Others will see what we have and will think, "I want that, too."

When I discovered the truth about sex and starting living it with my husband, it felt like this secret I could not keep to myself. Women who finish the Awaken-Love class can't wait to tell their friends. People are starved for real intimacy and they are looking for answers.

It makes me think about Jesus as he commissioned His disciples before he left them. They could not wait to tell others about Jesus. When you find an answer, you cannot keep it to yourself! I pray that you have found an answer.

We start changing the world by changing ourselves!

## Final Thoughts

The first year God called me to teach sex classes He gave me this verse: "But you have made me as strong as a wild ox. You have anointed me with the finest oil" (Psalm 92:10). Afterwards, I wrote this prayer:

> *Father God, fill me with your strength and your power. Give me a stubbornness that will not be broken. Make me wild for pursuing you and your calling in my life. Help me to live on the wild side, not worried about what the world thinks, but focused on you. God, you have anointed me with oil. You anointed me, you commissioned me, you have blessed me. God, when you are with me, I can accomplish all things. You have anointed me. I will not be afraid, I will not be weak, I will not give up. I am yours.*

**Like me, God has made you as strong as a wild ox. Now go and change the world!**

# Resource List

## Christian Books About Sex in Marriage

- **Sheet Music**: *Uncovering the Secrets of Sexual Intimacy in Marriage* by Dr. Kevin Leman
- **The Sexually Confident Wife**: *Connecting with Your Husband Mind Body Heart Spirit* by Shannon Ethridge
- **Hot, Holy, and Humorous**: *Sex in Marriage by God's Design* by J. Parker
- **The Good Girl's Guide to Great Sex** by Sheila Wray Gregoire

## Secular Books About Sexual Technique

- **She Comes First**: *The Thinking Man's Guide to Pleasuring a Woman* by Ian Kerner
- **The Big O**: *How to Have Them, Give Them, and Keep Them* by Lou Paget
- **The Elusive Orgasm**: *A Woman's Guide to Why She Can't and How She Can Orgasm* by Vivienne Cass

## Books for Sexual Healing

- **The Fantasy Fallacy**: *Exposing the Deeper Meaning Behind Sexual Thoughts* by Shannon Ethridge
- **Healing the Wounded Heart**: *The Heartache of Sexual Abuse and the Hope of Transformation* by Dan B. Allender

- **Shattered Vows**: *Hope and Healing for Women Who Have Been Sexually Betrayed* by Debra Laaser
- **Surfing for God**: *The Divine Desire Beneath Sexual Struggle* by Michael John

## Talking to Your Kids About Sex

- **How Babies are Made** by Steven Schepp and Andrew Andry
- **God's Design for Sex** by Stan and Brenna Jones
- **Good Pictures Bad Pictures**: *Porn-proofing Today's Young Kids* by Kristen A. Henson, MA and Gail Poyner, PhD
- **Talking to Your Kids About Sex**: *How to Have a Lifetime of Age-Appropriate Conversations with Your Children About Healthy Sexuality* by Mark Laaser, PhD

## Christian Marriage Websites

- **Awaken-Love**: www.awaken-love.net
- **Authentic Intimacy**: www.authenticintimacy.com
- **Hot, Holy and Humorous**: www.hotholyhumorous.com
- **Intimacy in Marriage**: www.intimacyinmarriage.com
- **The Forgiven Wife**: www.forgivenwife.com
- **The Generous Wife**: www.the-generous-wife.com
- **The Marriage Bed**: www.themarriagebed.com
- **To Love Honor and Vacuum**: www.tolovehonorandvacuum.com

# ABOUT THE AUTHOR

Ruth Buezis, founder of Awaken-Love, is not delivering the same old lines, half-truths, and lies about intimacy, sex, and marriage!

Through hours of studying the Bible, reading nearly every available book and blog about sex and marriage, and listening to other women tell their stories, Ruth has developed a curriculum and conversation that is changing marriages the world over.

Ruth's own perspective and marriage were transformed as she uncovered God's truths about sex and marriage while spending eight weeks studying Song of Songs. In 2012, she taught her first class on sex and intimacy to eight close friends. From that, Awaken-Love was born. Currently, over 1000 women have taken her class. Recently, Ruth has also developed classes for men and engaged couples. Leading a team of teachers, Ruth continues to teach, but also spends time writing and speaking at large group events.

Ruth has been married to her husband, Jim, for 30 years, and is a mother to four grown daughters. As a wife, mother, teacher, speaker, blogger, and author, Ruth leads by example - pursuing God's best for herself as an individual and in her marriage.

Made in the USA
Coppell, TX
18 September 2022

83342599R00144